MY MISADVENTURES AND FAILURES

(LAUGH OUT LOUD)

ASIM PANDYA
ADVOCATE (SENIOR!)

Dedicated

To

All who taught me life lessons

Contents

Contents

Part-II

My Unplanned Journey in Law Profession

Contents

Prologue

Before revealing what inspired me to write this book, I want to pose a question for you to stop and think about. The question is:

Can outstandingly naïve and bad decisions, misjudgements, and a headfirst dive into unknown territory lead to success?

My answer is 'YES', it can.

I know you're thinking that I am probably stupid. Oh, wait till you read the book! At least for me, it has so happened!

While many people write stories of success, autobiographies, or biographies of successful people to showcase what made them successful, you'll hardly find someone like me exposing stories of personal and professional misadventures and having the courage to open up only to be a subject matter of fun for the readers of this book. Well, that is the point. I am here to narrate the comedy of errors and misjudgements, which is my life which, I consider to be successful.

Who doesn't like to laugh at others' failed judgements and mishaps? Ideally, no one should, but let's face it, most of us do. The only difference is, some have the courage to laugh openly, while some do it behind others' backs. But here I am laughing at my own life, so you too are free to laugh. The purpose of this book is to entertain everyone, make them smile and normalise failures because I believe success can't be attained without failing miserably multiple times. The book will also reveal some unknown or less known but interesting facts of our judicial system and legal profession in a lighter tone but requiring serious consideration.

I am not oblivious to the fact that many people have faced much more adverse situations in life and surpassed those difficulties to become successful. In my view, there are far more successful people in the world. My success is absolutely insignificant in that context. In my profession, there are also many instances of first-generation lawyers coming from very poor and humble backgrounds and carving out a niche in the profession. So, I am no different. The only difference between them and me is that they have chosen not to share their life struggles with you, whereas I chose to write them down and share with all of you.

The idea of writing a memoir struck my mind one day while I was looking at my past and the experiments I did with my life. With all humility I do not proclaim that my life is a super success which could be an inspiration to others. But I do feel successful because the life I am living today is a dream for more than 99 percent of the Indian population. Fortunately, I have robust health, reasonable wealth, an unfathomable reservoir of exuberance, and rock-solid social support from my family and friends. I am happy that despite my follies and many outstandingly bad decisions I had taken at one or another stage of life, I could achieve this much in the profession of law and my life.

The individual characteristics that helped me sustain in the profession of law and reach the present position are hard work (now passion for law), courage, and perseverance. I am glad that I could flourish in the profession without sacrificing the quality of being truthful to my clients, to the court, and to my opponent lawyers. I, therefore, feel fortunate for whatever I have with the blessings of my parents and God (to me an unknown energy as I am an atheist).

Since I am an atheist, leaving the course of my life and my destiny in the hands of God was not an option available to me. Whatever I have achieved, if you consider it to be an achievement, is a result of my choices, right or wrong. Momentarily, I got bogged down by some unwanted situations, difficulties, or unexpected problems of life, but I was quite resilient to adjust to such difficulties, situations, or problems of life very quickly. I do not make complaints or fret over anything that happens to me or my family because life has blessed me with all luxuries, the best family, and the best friends. I have accepted the vicissitudes of life happily. In the aforesaid backdrop, I thought why not share my hilarious experiences and journey of life with all of you. Life is just a celebration for me, so just be part of this celebration while reading this book.

I would like to add a caveat that please do not misunderstand this book to be my autobiography. With all humility, I acknowledge that I do not belong to the group of individuals who are expected or justified to write their autobiographies. Writing an autobiography is a tough job. It means opening every page of your life for public view, which is conspicuously missing in this book. It is thus just a memoir delineating some laughable stuff. One can say that it is a smile(o)-graphy not a biography. It is just like a joy ride and to be enjoyed without being serious. It reveals how my naïve mind perceived the world during my childhood, young days, and even after growing in age. This proves the fact that age does not necessarily bring maturity in every case. How stupid my certain decisions were at some stages of life, or one may say to be full of divine wisdom, I do know!

Be that as it may, those stupid or wise actions, experiments or decisions have made my life full of thrill. I have not felt boredom for a single moment in my life. It is said that most of the people are dead at the age of thirty, but they are buried later when they physically perish. I am happy to report that I am still alive metaphorically and physically also. I still take decisions without much planning and enjoy the outcome whether good or bad. Somehow, my life has been influenced and propelled by one statement of Osho which goes like this: "Do not call it insecurity, call it freedom. Do not call it uncertainty, call it wonder".

I am truly blessed because my beloved family—my wife Ragini and my daughter Shaivaa—have shown steadfast allegiance and unconditional support in every decision of my life. Did my setbacks affect them? Yes, but they accepted it with as much enthusiasm and positivity as I did. I can't thank them enough for always being by my side. I am deeply beholden to my parents Jayant Pandya and Raseshwari Pandya who instilled courage in me to take charge of life and to face the world in my own way without thrusting upon me their perceptions of life and their experiences. I would like to express my heartfelt gratitude to my brothers, sister, cousins, friends, my colleagues in the profession and most importantly to my detractors in the profession who made my life thrilling, joyful, rich and fulfilling.

My goal in writing this book will be achieved if reading it compels you to smile. I am sure the book will certainly reduce your stress and help you accept failures as lessons. For my friends and family, the first part of the book will be of great interest, while for my friends in the profession, judges, and law students, the second part will generate more interest. For readers who do not know me personally, both parts may be of some interest or neither! But I am sure that this book will be of some use, even if not considered worth reading by small street vendors selling snacks as wrapping material or ragpickers as recyclable trash!

– Asim Pandya

———◈◈◈———

Part-I

———◈◈◈———

My Formative or
Say (De)Formative Years!

Chapter 1

An Illusion of a Divine Birth and My Family

On 26th July 1965 in a small village named Umreth in District Kheda of Gujarat at seven in the evening, it was raining heavily and the electricity supply got snapped. It was pitch dark and during this, my mother got labour pain. She was taken to the nearby hospital. At 7.15 p.m., I was born and coincidentally the electricity supply got restored. This incident was narrated by my mother when I grew up. This instilled a belief in my mind that like many spiritual souls who took humanity to a higher level or world leaders, I was also a divine soul born to lead the world from darkness to light. I grew up with the same illusion that I had taken birth on this planet to do great works and for the emancipation of miserable worldly people. This myth was broken in the later stage of my youth days as I noticed that I was less than an average person, nay a divine person.

For almost thirty years of my life, I have failed to understand why I was born in the village Umreth. I am expressing this surprise as my entire family, either from my father's side or my mother's side, had no connection with this village! My father, Jayant Maganlal Pandya, and my mother, Raseshwari Mahendra Desai, were both from the small town Dahod of District Panchmahal. My mother was from a very educated family. My mother's father, Mahendra Desai, was a well-known lawyer in Dahod and a freedom fighter. My father's father (my grandfather), Maganlal Pandya, was a headmaster in a primary school and stayed in Ramji Temple in the Padav area of Dahod. I was under the misconception until recently that the said Ramji Temple belonged to my grandfather and was owned by us. The temple was on the ground floor, and my grandfather would stay in the house-like structure on the first floor surrounding the dome of the temple. Of late, I came to know that it was not owned by us. My grandfather possessed hereditary rights of *Pujari* (worshipper) in the temple! So, we belong to the Pujari lineage, and the paradox is that my father and we all turned out to be atheists despite being in the company of God!

It was just a divine coincidence that I was born in the village with which I had no family ties or remotest connection.

I came to know much later in my life the reason for my birth in Umreth. The reason was that my father Jayant Pandya got a job as a professor in Dakor College in the town known as Dakor before my birth. Dakor is approximately ten kilometres away from the village Umreth. The Dakor College was on the outskirts of Dakor town on the highway and at an equal distance from the village Umreth and Dakor. I think my parents did not find a suitable home at a reasonable rent in Dakor and hence they possibly chose Umreth as their temporary home. Beyond the fact that I was born in Umreth I have no connection with that place and have no feelings of belongingness for that town.

I do not have any memory of the first five years of my life. I have a faint memory that after some time my parents shifted to Mehmdavad and while we were staying in Mehmdavad, my father decided to go to London. I do not know what prompted my father to go to London, but I believe that he went for further study. I came to know that he went to London even though he had not enough money. He went to London with 8 UK Pounds, struggled and stayed there for two to three years. Judging by my nature and behavioural pattern, it seems that the trait of doing whatever my mind thinks appropriate has been genetically derived from my father. My father came back from London somewhere in the years 1969-70. I have not verified it, but I was told that my father did his Masters in English in London.

My family consisted of my father Jayant Pandya, my mother Raseshwari Desai-Pandya, my sister Nandini, my brother Ashesh, and myself. I am the youngest son of my parents. I am not bothering you with the details of my forefathers since I am not a child of a king where it is relevant to state the ancestry.

I have very little memory of our home in Mehmdavad. Nothing significant happened in Mehmdavad except I fell down once while taking a bath and got a serious injury on my head. That injury is still visible on the back portion of my head.

By the time I reached the age of 5 or 6, our family shifted to Ahmedabad. In Ahmedabad, we started staying in a rented house in the colony known as professor's colony, which was situated at the end of the western part of Ahmedabad. There were no proper roads to reach our home in those days. Proper roads were there up to Gujarat University Bus-stand only. As said earlier, my father came back from London just one or two years before we started staying in Ahmedabad. My father brought a spool-player of Grundig Company from Germany. I am still surprised why he brought that music player and recorder as he had no great interest in music. He probably brought it because he had recorded poetries written by him in his own voice and loving messages for the family while he was in London far away from us. My father's poetry recitation was amazing. I have hardly heard anyone reciting poetries and verses in Sanskrit so beautifully like my father. My father also brought a mixer grinder in those days from London, some photographs, and a doll-like toy of a British Royal Guard wearing a red coat, black trousers, and a black furry hat. Somehow, my father had a great influence of Britishers in his mind as he happened to stay in London for approximately three years. He, therefore, brought British culture with him to some extent, and we rustics like Indians were introduced to that culture. But I, my brother, and sister were never impressed with that culture as we disdained discipline, speaking softly, and remaining properly groomed all the time. My father was at the same time influenced by Mahatma Gandhi's philosophy. So, he would wear only Khadi clothes but properly starched and ironed. His hair was always neatly combed. My mother was a simple, honest, and down-to-earth woman. She had no demands in her life. I was always opposite to my father in every aspect of living. My father introduced bread, butter, cheese, jam, eggs, cornflakes, etc., to our family when these things were not known to the majority of the Indian population. My mother was a teacher in school. My father was a part-time professor in a college as he frequently left the teaching job for one reason or another. Thus, essentially our family was dependent on my mother's salary, which was not sufficient to cater to the needs of the family of five members. I remember that in the last week of every month, my mother would start complaining that her salary had been exhausted, but fortunately, the provision store owner would give us groceries on credit. It was indeed a contradiction that despite meagre family income, my father would not hesitate to spend money on good food items and fruits. But when the question of spending money on furniture, clothing, and other necessary home items would arise, he would say that we could not afford such items. My father used to smoke fifteen to twenty cigarettes every day.

My father was very strict and disciplined in every sphere of life, including our upbringing. He disliked noise and people speaking loudly. He wanted us to follow his system of discipline, which we were not willing to follow. My father would lose his temper over the most trivial issues or the slightest deviation from the rules of discipline he had crafted for us. Everyone in our family was afraid of our father. My mother, too, was always scared of failing to maintain the schedule set by our father. She had not much freedom, and her schedule had to be according to my father's routine. In contrast, my mother was a virtuous woman. She was always calm and would never lose her temper. We children had never been scolded by our mother. She was a perfect human being. My mother always tried to shield us from the wrath of our father. So, I, my sister Nandini, and my brother Ashesh were brought up in two extremes, like the North Pole and the South Pole.

At the age of nine, I came to know that I have a uterine brother named Nishith Desai. My mother's marriage with our father was her second marriage. My mother's first marriage was with one Madan Desai. I was told by my mother that Madan Desai had a heart problem. Madan Desai tried to persuade my mother not to marry him because of his heart problem as he knew that he would not live longer. My mother gently told Madan Desai that she was dealing with a human being she loved and not any goods to be rejected because of a defect in it. She made it clear to Madan Desai that she would not reject her love merely because her loved one had a problem in his heart. Madan Desai and my mother both knew that their journey together would be short. Despite that, my mother insisted that both should marry, and both got married. Out of their wedlock, a son was born in the year 1950 who was given the name Nishith. Within a short span thereafter, Madan Desai died, and my mother became a widow. My mother was 27 or 28 years of age. After six to seven years of the death of Madan Desai, because of the insistence and pressure of her friends and well-wishers, she was persuaded to marry a second time. In those days, a second marriage was a taboo. My mother was well-educated and a reformist. She was working as a teacher in those days, and there she came in contact with Jayant Pandya, my father. My mother and Jayant Pandya had some common friends, and one of them was a couple named Pradyumna Bhatt and Kusum Bhatt. This couple persuaded my mother and father to get married. My father was also a reformist and agreed to marry a widow, my mother. The second marriage of my mother was opposed by the parents of my mother, but against the wishes of her parents Mahendra Desai and Premlatta Desai (our maternal grandparents), she married Jayant Pandya. Because of this fact, the parents of my mother snapped their relations with my mother for a considerable long time. In the year 1960, my sister Nandini was born. So, my mother, father, Nishith, and my sister Nandini started staying together as a family. As said earlier, my father had a bad temper, and on account of the birth of Nandini, frictions started between my mother and my father about the usual love, care, and nurturing of Nishith, the son of my mother from the first marriage of my mother. My father would not mind beating his child as in those days it was quite usual. It seems that for small things he would scold Nishith or sometimes beat him. We had also been beaten by our father many times during our childhood and youth days. In our time, even teachers had the liberty to beat a student as it was believed that "spare the rod and spoil the child". But it seems that my mother felt that Nishith was treated unfairly by our father because he was his stepson, and we do not know she might be right in her belief. My mother had to remain a mute spectator to the routine scolding and ill-treatment given to Nishith by our father. We believe that things must have gone from bad to worse. Finally, my mother was left with no choice but to send Nishith to Bombay to his paternal aunt's home to avoid daily frictions in the family. My mother had no choice of going back to her parents as the second marriage was against the wishes of her parents. Finally, under compulsion of the circumstances, Nishith at the age of ten or eleven was sent to her paternal aunt's home in Bombay. My mother had guilt throughout her life of sending Nishith to Bombay and depriving him of the love, care, and affection of the mother in his formative years. My mother admitted several times when we grew up that she wanted Nishith to be saved from the everyday frictions and disputes that arose in the family after the birth of my sister. I must say that it was my father's usual nature to flare up and beat his children to keep them in discipline. But a stepson would take it differently, and hence my mother sent Nishith away from her with a heavy heart.

My father had many good qualities. He possessed impeccable honesty and integrity. He was a man of literature, a political thinker-analyst, and reformist. He was active in the Congress Party and General Secretary of Gujarat Pradesh Congress Committee. The late Prime Minister Ms. Indira Gandhi knew my father personally and would call my father by his last name. My father's love for his children remained mostly hidden inside him and would rarely surface. I would not like to talk about my father in detail as it is beside the point in this book. The most important contribution of our father in our life was that he would never thrust upon us his ideologies or his dreams. He kept us in discipline but gave us complete freedom of thought and taking charge of our life. I must mention that my mother, through her unconditional love, taught us lessons of compassion, empathy, kindness, simplicity, and honesty. My mother pampered all her three children. Only because of her love and understanding of our needs could we avoid taking a wrong path in life. In her life, she had no enemies, and I have never heard anyone speaking badly about my mother even during gossip.

My brother Ashesh was born in the year 1964 and I was born in the year 1965 just within a span of one and a half years. I sometimes asked my mother about the necessity of bringing me to this planet as in those days *"Hum do aur hamare do"* was the slogan of the government. Once a baby boy and a baby girl are there in the family, nobody would usually bring a third child. My mother candidly replied that when she became pregnant for the third time, she did not realise that she was pregnant. She thought she was passing through menopause and that her menstrual cycle stopped due to menopause as she was 40 years old when I was in her womb. But when she consulted a doctor, it was revealed that it was me inside the womb which had led her menstrual cycle to stop temporarily. Possibly this was discovered very late and hence there was no chance of terminating her pregnancy. So, I was a product of an accident and not a conscious choice of my parents. However, after my birth, I was given the highest love and affection by my parents. I was the most pampered child by my parents.

I was born with a small defect in one eye. The eyelids of both my eyes were not equal in length. One eyelid was a little longer than the other one. So, my parents decided to get surgery done at Civil Hospital Ahmedabad as there was no concept of a private hospital in those days. The surgery was successful, but the scar and the defect remained visible if someone looked closely at me. Because of this defect, which I came to know during my school days, I was subjected to banter by other students. I developed an inferiority complex. I subconsciously started blinking my eyes frequently to avoid the defect being noticed. This inferiority complex remained with me until I got married and became successful in life to some extent. My wife, Ragini, drew my attention to this point after our marriage, and thereafter, I tried to overcome this issue consciously. Whether or not I have overcome this eye-blinking habit, only you all can say!

I spent my childhood and youth days in professor's Colony in Navarangpura area of Ahmedabad city. Initially in flat No. 30, a rented premises. After some years, when my mother's parents pardoned my mother for her second marriage and accepted her family, with some financial help from my mother's parents, we purchased flat No. 50 in the same colony, an owned house. Flat No. 50 remained my home until the year 1995-96 when, after marriage, I started my own family and lived separately.

I have many fond memories of my childhood and school days in Professors' Colony. I will narrate only a few important events from those memories.

Chapter 2

Studying in a Girls' School and Changing Schools for Flimsy Reasons

When I was 5 years old, I was admitted to Balmandir (Kindergarten) named Parijat School near our home in Professors' Colony. After Balmandir, I was admitted to a girls' school named Bhakt Vallabh Dhola Primary and Secondary School situated in Maninagar area near Shah e Alam. It was not that there was some problem with my gender, and I was admitted to a girls' school. It was because my mother was a teacher in that girls' school and there was a policy of the management of the school to permit male kids up to 3rd standard to study in their girls' school so that the female teachers can look after their child if they are studying in the same school where they teach. That school was almost one hour's distance by bus from our home. The concept of a school bus was not in vogue in those days. So, my mother and I would walk every day for fifteen minutes from our home to catch an AMTS (Ahmedabad Municipal Transport Service) bus from Gujarat University Bus-stand. While returning home, we would follow the same routine. We would get down at Gujarat University Bus-stand and walk again for fifteen minutes. On many days, my mother and I would walk from Shah e Aalam crossroads to Majoor Gam to buy reasonably priced vegetables and take a bus from Geeta Mandir bus-stand. Thus, from my childhood, walking became part of my life. I will share my walking experiences in a later chapter. The only important memory of my studying at Bhakt Vallabh Dhola School was that in an examination, I was asked to write an essay on a Cow. The question was "Please write an essay in five to ten lines on the animal Cow". Fortunately, I did not go to find out a Cow and write something about it. But I thought that there must be some hidden meaning in the aforementioned question. My understanding of language was not good at the age of six years. So, I calculated from five to ten and found that I had to write five lines only in the essay. I wrote only five lines though I could have written more than ten lines. It was the first instance of my stupidity, or you may say analytical skill! The second incident that I remember is that I got 5 marks in the subject maths out of 50!

After studying in a girls' school up to 3rd standard, I was required to be admitted to another school. My father and mother, though in the field of teaching, did not use their influence to get me admission to any reputed school, or it is quite possible that they might not be influential. I wanted to study in C. N Vidyalaya or A.G Teacher's school, but it was not possible to get admission to those schools by transfer from another school. I was therefore admitted to Ishwar Bhavan School near our home. This school was only up to 5th standard. I studied in Ishwar Bhavan for two years. In Ishwar Bhavan, I made three good friends named Tapan Mehta, Umang Pandya, and Bhaumik Jani. The school was barely eight hundred metres away from our home, so I was a little bit relieved from walking fifteen minutes I used to walk while studying in Bhakt Vallabh Dhola School.

After 6th standard, the question arose again as to which school now? My father asked me to choose a school as if I had many choices. I chose a school named Ramanuj School because one of my friends from Professors' Colony named Ashok Gandalal Patel was studying there. It was a school housed in a small residential bungalow. It was not a well-maintained building. There was no concept of hygiene or cleanliness. Like Bhakt Vallabh Dhola School, the toilets were stinking with a foul smell. There was no concept of flushing after urination or defecation. Most of the time, the water taps remained dry. For drinking water also, the school had a common water tank or a huge earthen pot, and God knows whether the tank/pot was ever cleaned by the staff of the school management! Be that as it may, in this filthy environment, I did not fall sick. In Ramanuj School, I did not enjoy a bit. In that school, there was a menace of flies (insects). The flies would constantly sit on the face, hands, or legs. The situation would get aggravated by the small vendors standing outside the school building selling chopped masala cucumbers, tomatoes, amboliya, amla, and unbranded orange candies in an open *laary* (a handcart with four wheels). I got fed up with the flies' menace and the unhealthy environment of the school. So, I declared before my father that I did not want to study in Ramanuj School. My father asked me why I was not willing to go to that school. I said that there was a nuisance of flies in the school and that I did not like the school. My father said fine. My father then asked me, "which school now?" I said Nutan Fellowship School. This school was situated off Ashram Road towards Sabarmati River. I opted for this school because a friend, Jagdish Kachrabhai Patel (his father Kacharabhai became Kanchanbhai later on upon changing his name), was studying in that school. In Nutan School, students were mainly from the Muslim Society, Navrangpura Gam, Khanpur, and Shahpur areas of Ahmedabad. Most of the students were from the poor or lower-middle strata of society and would come barefoot. Some would wear rubber slippers. Anyone wearing shoes was a rare scene in Nutan School. This school was situated 5 km away from my home in Professors' Colony. My parents would give me 40 paisa for the AMTS bus fare for reaching school and the return journey. My friend Jagdish teasingly addressed as Jago or Jaglo was not fortunate to get bus fare from his father. So, he and his brother Bipin also known as Biplo would walk to school every day from their home situated in our society. I, therefore, decided to walk 5 km to school and 5 km back home with Jaglo and Biplo. Two more students would join us from the nearby society. We all would wear rubber slippers on our feet and walk briskly in unison, creating a symphony (systematic noise) fataak…fataak…fataak, and we would enjoy this noise. In this school, every evening there would be a free fight between one or the other group of students over some petty issues, sometimes on issues like following a girl student or teasing a girl student or staring at a girl student by a male student. A crowd of passersby would gather near the school gate to watch the fights free of cost and entertain themselves.

In the period of games/Physical Training, we students would play with a big-sized rubber ball which could not be said to be a volleyball or football in open space (not a playground) near Sabarmati River. Some of us would deliberately kick the rubber ball into the river, and then all boys would jump into the river to get the ball back. I must mention that the river was never flowing from one bank to the other bank. Only a small stretch of the river contained water up to four-five feet. It was more like a rivulet. After taking a bath in the river under the pretext of finding the ball, we would sit in class with water-soaked clothes. Our teachers were absolutely unconcerned with what students do. They did not even notice that the students were sitting with wet clothes. In Nutan School, I made two best friends. One was Islam Nizamuddin Kalavant, and the second was Jiyauddin Nuruddin Kadari. We enjoyed our friendship and spent a considerable time together during my two years in Nutan School. I, for the first time, tasted non-vegetarian food in their company. I have narrated that experience in a separate chapter. My days in Nutan School were full of fun and thrill.

From 8th standard to 12th, for the first time in my life, I studied in one school known as Ankur High School and Higher Secondary

School for five long years continuously. I do not remember how I got admission to Ankur School. Most likely, since it was a secondary school, I had the chance to shift from primary school to a new secondary school. The school was situated near Gandhigram Railway Station. It was housed in a commercial-type four-storied building. It was a decent school compared to my previous schools. The school uniform consisted of a white shirt with a badge and sky-blue denim shorts. The badge had a symbol and below it, "Play the Game" were inscribed. The paradox was that the school had no playground at all, whereas the badge contained the words "Play the Game". During games/PT periods, we students would be either taken to the terrace or to Gujarat College Ladies Hostel Ground, which was one kilometre away from the school. I was neither good at any sports nor in studies, but I enjoyed my friendships with new friends in this decent school. In Ankur School, I made many friends. Some of them were Chetan Shah, Dharmesh Shah, Himanshu Thaker, Nagesh Pathak, Rupal Shah, Partish Parikh, Chirag Desai (now Dr. Chirag Desai), Nikesh Shah, Yogesh Panchal, Bharat Joshi, Sajid Sheikh, and Munavvar Pathan, etc. One Shivkumar Joshi was also my friend, whose father had a tea stall at Gandhigram Railway, and I felt proud of being his friend, who had a tea stall at the railway station. I was very shy and diffident; hence, I had no courage to talk to girls. So, I had no girlfriend in my school days, and I still regret that I could not make a single girlfriend.

I used to bunk my classes during my school days in Ankur. Himanshu Thaker, my school friend, and I would go to watch movies. I stealthily went to watch many movies without informing my parents during school hours or after school. In ninth standard, I found the subject of maths most troublesome. I did not understand algebra at all. Therefore, I requested my friend, Pratish Parikh, during the final examination of maths to allow me to copy from his answer paper. I copied from somebody else's paper only once in my life. He got 36 out of 50 marks, and I got 37 out of 50 marks in the maths paper, and I passed my 9th standard. I probably got one mark more for my better handwriting; otherwise, the answer contained material copied from Pratish Parikh. Later on, Pratish became an engineer, which he deserved. I became a lawyer, that too with great difficulties when left with no other career options.

Chapter 3

The Earth is Round; I Re-Established This Truth

While I was studying in 5th Standard at Ishwar Bhavan School, we were once taught by our teacher, Gandhi Saheb, that the earth is round. Therefore, if we start walking from any one point, in the end, we complete a full circle and reach the same point from where we started. I took this literally. During our vacation, when we visited our maternal grandparents' home in Dahod, I told my brother, Ashesh, and my cousin, Mihir, about what I had learnt in school. I mentioned that the earth is round, and wherever you start walking, you eventually return to the same location. The next morning at 6 o'clock, my brother, Ashesh, cousin Mihir, and I set out for a walk from our grandparents' home in Dahod to test this theory in real life without informing anyone about our expedition. We headed towards the railway tracks of the Dahod-Delhi railway line, where we found shiny black and white stones placed between the tracks. We were fascinated by these stones and collected some, thinking they were like diamonds. We had been taught that such stones could be used to ignite a fire by striking one against the other, creating friction that would spark a flame. We attempted to burn some pieces of paper scattered near the railway tracks with these shiny stones by striking them together. However, we could not ignite a fire or even see a spark when the stones collided. We assumed that a spark or fire might not be visible during the daytime. We kept some stones in our shorts' pockets and held others in our hands as we walked for three hours, hoping to return to our starting point. Fortunately, after three hours, we re-entered Dahod town from the opposite end. Meanwhile, back at our grandparents' home, our mother and maternal aunts discovered that the three of us were missing. They began searching in all directions, fearing we had been abducted, or something had happened to us. They sent our other cousins to look for us and were on the verge of reporting us missing to the police. However, before they could do so, we arrived home, completely exhausted and sweaty. Upon our return, we were greeted with slaps from our maternal aunt (Mihir's mother). The stones we held in our hands fell to the ground, and tears streamed down our cheeks. We were scolded by everyone present at home. Despite all three of us crying and shocked by the sudden slaps and unwelcome reception, I felt a little happy inside, as my theoretical understanding of the earth's roundness had been proven and firmly established in real life.

Chapter 4

My First Experience of Eating Non-Vegetarian

During my school days at Nutan School, I had two Muslim friends named Jiyauddin Kadari and Islam Kalavant. As mentioned earlier, eggs were introduced into our family's daily diet by our father due to British influence. We mainly consumed boiled eggs, with omelettes being a rare occurrence. Having befriended two Muslim classmates, I became curious about trying non-vegetarian food. I expressed this curiosity to my father, who was not keen on the idea. He believed that the eggs we ate were non-fertile, hence consuming them did not involve violence. However, when I sought his permission to try non-vegetarian dishes, he disapproved, quoting someone who said, "My stomach is not a graveyard." He provided several reasons for his stance during a thirty-minute discussion, attempting to dissuade me from pursuing non-vegetarian food. Despite his efforts, my inquisitive mind, eager to explore new tastes, remained undeterred. My father began to dislike my Muslim friends, wrongly attributing my interest in non-vegetarian food to their influence. After some time, I confided in Jiyauddin and Islam about my desire to sample non-vegetarian cuisine. A few days later, Jiyauddin discreetly brought two pieces of partially cooked non-vegetarian food to school, hidden in his shorts pocket. During recess, he took me aside and offered me a taste. The flavour was unpleasant, and I promptly spat it out, fighting the urge to vomit. Disappointed by the experience, I informed Islam, who agreed that the semi-cooked offering was not the proper way to introduce someone to non-vegetarian food. Islam promised to invite me to his home to try authentic non-vegetarian dishes, particularly mentioning their delicious fish preparations. After a month of anticipation, I received the eagerly awaited invitation from Islam, providing his address in a bungalow located in Muslim Society near Navrangpura railway crossing. Upon reaching his home, I noticed a makeshift hut in the corner of the compound, where Islam resided. Adjacent to the hut, a cot with jute strings stood, with a tethered goat nearby. Islam greeted me warmly and invited me to sit on the cot. He emerged from his home with a bowl of cooked fish, urging me to taste it. Uncertain about the protocol, I expected bread or chapati alongside the fish. Sensing my confusion, Islam brought a roti in an aluminium dish. He demonstrated how to eat the fish by removing a bone from the oily red gravy and savouring the dish. Following his lead, I tentatively tried the fish, realising it only contained one bone. Overcoming my initial hesitation, I managed to eat a small portion of the fish. This experience was an improvement from my first encounter with non-vegetarian food, which involved the unappetising semi-cooked meat from Jiyauddin's pocket. I learnt that Islam's father was a Sarangi Player at the radio station, earning a modest income.

During my school days at Nutan School, these two dear friends would sometimes take me to Navrangpura Mosque, which was nearby our school, for eating Khichado, a food item cooked with pulses and paddy/ rice. Usually, on all Fridays, Khichado would be served free of charge to everyone coming to the mosque. It would be served in one common aluminium plate for the three of us. We would go to the terrace-type open area of the mosque and eat Khichado from the common aluminium plate. Although Khichado served in the mosque was a vegetarian dish, it contained mutton pieces. My two friends by then knew that I did not like non-veg much. So, they would take out mutton pieces from Khichado and throw them in the air one after the other for the consumption of crows waiting there on the terrace for the littered food. Crows would catch a mutton piece while it is in the air. We would enjoy watching this unique scene and laugh childishly.

Because of my friendship with these two friends, I would reach home late. One day I was late by more than two hours to reach home. I was welcomed by my father with slaps and was then beaten with a stick. My father was fuming with anger and felt that I was being spoiled by these two friends. He complained to the Principal of the School and asked the principal to keep me away from the company of these friends. I was scolded by the principal and punished by being told to stand outside the classroom for two days. After the punishment was over, she advised me to keep my distance from these two boys. But I hardly paid any heed to her advice. We remained good friends until I changed my school. My experience of studying in Nutan School was full of aimless loitering, thrill, and joy. Thereafter, I started eating non-veg when I was in college. Sometimes I liked it, sometimes I did not. Now, I am not very fond of non-veg and avoid eating it as far as possible. Jiyauddin is still my friend and meets me whenever he has legal work or wants legal advice. Islam was also in touch with me during Saptak Music Festival arranged by the Saptak School of Music every year as he was from a musicians' family and someone from his family would be performing in the music festival. He was found sitting outside the music hall talking to music artists and passing his time. Islam became rich after leaving study, and his family owned a hotel named Poonam Palace in Ahmedabad. But three to four years back, I got the news of his untimely death at the age of 55.

Chapter 5

Mission Fox and My Days in Professors' Colony

In Nutan School, as stated above, the scenario was one of purposeless and nonchalant loitering with my Muslim friends. In our residential society, also, the routine was just to keep playing different Indian games, namely, running and driving cycle tyres with a stick, playing *Bhammardo* (wooden cock), Marble, *Indu, Kabaddi, Sankal Sat Taali, Maldudi, King, Thappo and Langdi.* Cricket had not entered our life until my best friend Mehul Sheth came to stay in our society in the year 1977-78. Most of the time we boys of the society were found playing in the common plot, where there was a big tree of *Peepli* (a kind of tree), not a Pipal tree. We were fond of climbing that tree and reaching the highest branch. During hot summer days, the aforesaid tree was our cooler. At noon, we would climb the tree and stay on the branches like monkeys. If we felt hungry, we would eat the leaves of *Peepli* like goats. We would make *Pipudi* (a sound-creating instrument which goes peee…puuu…peee…puuu…) of its leaves and playfully jump here and there on the tree or under the tree. We fell down many times and got injured on legs and hands. Whenever there was any bruise, abrasion, or small wound on our legs, our ready and instant medical aid was our own urine. We would urinate on the injured portion of the limb and get recovered. If our arm or leg got twisted or dislocated, our saviour was Vaid Narhari Prasad's clinic opposite V.S. Hospital. He was an expert in curing twisted or dislocated hands or legs. He would twist the limb in the opposite direction and then apply pink and brown lotion to the injured part. We would get cured in fifteen days or three weeks.

We would drink water from a tap situated anywhere in the society or the garden near our society. Since my mother and father both were working, my brother and I had plenty of time to waste on useless pursuits. In those days in the university area where we stayed, foxes and jackals were also sighted occasionally. Once, my brother, my friend named Paresh Dave, and I found a fox in the university area, near Botany School. Our minds full of energy and ready for adventures decided to capture the fox. The next day, my brother Ashesh, my friend Paresh Dave, and I gathered at one place in the society, took a long stick, a small knife, and a rope for capturing a fox. Some aunts of our society, watching us doing something fishy, asked us what we were doing. In reply, the three of us said that we were going on an adventure to capture a fox. They tried to persuade us not to go for such an adventure, but we were firm fools. We set out for our adventure, "the mission fox". We wandered here and there for three hours in the university area but could not find any fox. We found some stray dogs, but they were of no use to us as we wanted to catch a fox. We came back home tired, disheartened, and disappointed after three long hours. Our mission to catch a fox failed. People laughed at us as we returned empty-handed.

In those days when I was ten years old, I developed a friendship with a son of a vegetable vendor having a wooden cabin near our society for selling vegetables. His name was Maadhu but fondly called Maadhio. He and I became very good friends. When I had nothing to do, I would sit in his shop and take pride in selling vegetables as a proxy of my friend Madhio. He was really a good boy. Sometimes he would bring samosas for both of us, and we would relish samosas. Otherwise, cucumber and tomatoes were our regular snack items in his shop. There was a provision store adjoining his vegetable shop known as Patel Provision Store.

It was also a wooden cabin. The owner of the shop was one Patel uncle. His son Rasik was of my age. I had a friendship with him also. But he never offered a free candy or a peppermint to me. I remember taking care of his shop too but rarely. I used to take care of the vegetable shop of Madhiya regularly when he had gone for lunch or to buy vegetables. Madhiya had taken me to movies a couple of times paying from his pocket. He would prefer to take me to tax-free movies as the tickets of such movies were cheap. We remained very good friends for a long time until I entered college and made new friends. I still cherish my good memories of friendship with him.

After my best friend Mehul Sheth came to reside in our colony, cricket was introduced to us. He would play very good cricket whereas we others were average players. It was difficult to bowl him out. Gradually we started playing cricket with a match ball without safety guards. I made a new friend named Mayur Majithia when he came from Jamnagar and started staying with his sister in the same colony. He was also one of my best friends. He was a fast bowler and a good batsman. With Mehul and Mayur, the cricket team of Professors' Colony became very strong. We played many cricket matches with the teams of nearby societies where victory depended on these two players. I would make five to ten runs and get out. I was a wicketkeeper of the team and thought very highly of myself in wicketkeeping. But I was not a great wicketkeeper. My friend Mehul would take proper cricket coaching and narrate his experiences of playing in the stadium. I was fascinated by his narration of taking cricket coaching. I also thought of becoming a cricketer for a while, but I had no great skill. Above all, my father was unwilling to spend any amount on me and my brother. He saw no future for his sons in cricket or any other pursuit.

When I was in 10ᵗʰ Standard, I thought of joining the military. I expressed my desire to my friends and asked for their wishes. Some of them said they would also like to join the military. We decided to go to the military cantonment area where we found an office-like building as soon as we entered the military campus. We reached the military office barefoot, with uncombed hair, slovenly dressed in shorts and ordinary clothes. Someone sitting in the office looked at us with disdain and asked us the purpose of our visit. We could barely state the purpose of our visit as none of us was fluent in Hindi or English. In broken Hindi, one of us said that we wanted to join the army. The officer sitting there was bemused by our skinny appearance and foolish act of directly reaching the military office without knowing anything. We barefoot urchins were driven out by him without further conversation, saying *"bahgo salo…military join karana tumhara kaam nahi hai"* (Go back, you stupid boys, it is not your cup of tea to join the military). Our dream to join the military crumbled there and then. Still, the dream of joining the military kept haunting me. When I passed my 12ᵗʰ examination, I decided to appear in the Combined Defence Services Examination as one known person had in the past appeared in such an examination and cleared it. I started preparing for the CDS exams. I appeared but could not clear it. So, finally, I gave up the idea of joining the military forever. The aforementioned person known to me who was selected in the military later abandoned it. I do not know whether he was officially declared a deserter or not! But when I met that person next time in my life, he had joined the Forest Service in the State of Gujarat.

Chapter 6

Sporadic Attempts for Chasing Strong Health

During the school days, I was physically very weak, barely weighing 35 to 40 kg. Because of my habit of overeating and some other reasons, I had a runny nose throughout the year. At the age of ten or eleven, I constantly felt the urge to spit out the accumulated mucus in the throat. In fact, I was unable to withhold the phlegm gathered in the nose and throat. I would feel sheer embarrassment by first coughing like an old man of seventy and then spitting out the phlegm. One day, my mother and I were travelling to Dahod on a State Transport bus. I occupied the window seat so that if I had to spit out, it would be convenient. I started spitting out from the window during the running bus. Because of the speed of the bus and wind, whenever I spat, it would give a shower to the passengers sitting next to windows in the two seats behind me. One passenger got angry and told me not to spit out of the window. I had to control the urge of spitting for the next three hours until we reached Dahod. This and a few other similar instances saddened me. Some of my friends in society started teasing me, saying "Shembud Dada". I did not understand the meaning of the aforesaid word at that time. The word really meant a person having a runny nose. Having faced this kind of teasing and embarrassments routinely, I decided to do something to address this problem. In those days, in our study material, there was a chapter on *Pahelvan* (a bodybuilder, wrestler) Ram Murthy. He was also very weak, thin, and underweight in his childhood days. He was also ridiculed by his friends for being weak and thin. But he decided to overcome his weakness by doing exercises. He started going to the gym (*Akhada*). With sheer hard work, he became a renowned *Pahelvan* by successfully transforming his weak body into a strong body. He got fame at the national level. The story of *Pahelvan* Ram Murthy inspired me, and I also started doing exercises. I started with a walk for one hour every day. I gradually started running one kilometre and then started running five to six km every day. I was also very inspired by Karate and kung fu master Bruce Lee, so I brought his poster and pasted it in one room of our home. I brought one fighting instrument (weapon) known as "Nan-chak" used by Bruce Lee in his films. In his films, whenever a Nan-chak was wielded in circular motions by Bruce Lee, it would make some hissing noise. I started learning the art of wielding the Nan-chak. I, with hard work, increased the speed of wielding the Nan-chak. I reached forty cycles of wielding in circular motions with the hope that increasing the speed would create a hissing noise as heard in the films of Bruce Lee. While I was learning "Nan-chak" in the zest of increasing its speed, I hurt myself on hands and head many times, but I was not deterred by the hurts. But I was disappointed by the fact that while I was wielding the Nan-chak in circular motions, it did not create that hissing noise. I, therefore, started creating such noise through my mouth and became happy wielding the Nan-chak like Bruce Lee. Since I was very skinny, my friends started calling me "Khenkh Lee" (meaning an unusually thin and skinny person) in derision. When I grew a little older, I realised that it was just a sound effect used in the films. Else, even if Bruce Lee wielded the Nan-chak with whatever speed, it would not produce such a sound in reality.

I joined the gym known as Pritamnagar Akhada to build my body. The instructor was very strict, and he did not allow any newcomer to do weightlifting or use the bodybuilding instruments for three months until one's body gets ready for such hard tasks. I had no patience. I got bored doing small exercises as per the instructor's instructions. I lacked determination too. I gave it up in three to four months. I miserably failed. I learnt Yogasan and Pranayama too. I learnt various breathing techniques like Kapal Bhati, Bhastrika, Sutra Neti, Jal Neti, Uddiyana Bandha, and Nauli Kriya without difficulty. However, I could not stick to any one activity for long. So, I could neither build a stout body nor become an expert in Yoga. Be that as it may, the net outcome of all these efforts was that I could successfully overcome the physical compulsion of spitting out phlegm every ten to fifteen minutes. The benefit of this learning is that I can still do these breathing techniques and Yogasanas easily without much effort. Shirshasana, which is considered to be a difficult one, I still do without any support once or twice a week.

I did swimming also for a considerable long time but could not acquire enough speed to participate in a tournament. In the meantime, I started playing outdoor badminton from 12th standard. I became very passionate about my exercise regime and badminton. I had represented my college in badminton three consecutive years and participated in inter-college competitions. I had only once earned a bronze medal in the tournament held by the Ahmedabad Municipal Corporation forty years before. Beyond the above accomplishments, I have not achieved anything great in any sports. But now, I realise that though I did not excel in any of the activities, these activities did help me in achieving very good health. Today, at the age of sixty, I have no health issues with the grace of God. I still devote one hour every day to maintaining good health. Fortunately, I am not dependent on any medicine for keeping good health. I can still play singles games in badminton without difficulties. I participate in State and National level tournaments reaching quarter-finals or sometimes semi-finals at this age. I have seen that most of the people commit a mistake of running behind a career or money, ignoring the most important matter, i.e. health. I am trying to maintain a happy balance between my career, health, and family. It is indeed sad that people earn wealth at the cost of health to be able to afford the most expensive hospitals. I feel blessed and successful for not falling into the aforementioned category of people.

Chapter 7

Passion for Badminton and Debacles in Tournaments

As mentioned earlier, we started playing outdoor badminton in our society when I was in 12th Standard at school. Gradually, it became my passion. My friends and I were of the belief that we were champions and unbeatable. While we were labouring under that misconception, somebody said that badminton is usually played on indoor courts and not in the open air. I was a little surprised to know this fact since my world was very small. My friends and I, for the first time, went to see an inter-college tournament at NRS Hall of Gujarat University just within a month or two thereafter. It was a match between H L Commerce College and L. D. Engineering. The players were brilliant. We were taken aback by looking at the skill of the players. We realised that we knew nothing about badminton and were simply novices. After watching the badminton matches, we were more attracted to the game. We started searching for an indoor badminton court. One of us found out a badminton court in L D Engineering College campus. Unfortunately, none of us was studying at L D Engineering College. We found a big hole in one of the broken windows of the aforementioned badminton court. So, we started slipping in surreptitiously into the badminton court. The said badminton court had a slippery floor and a very low height. So, we would play flat badminton, oblivious to the concept of tossing a shuttlecock very high. The concept of a high service or tossing, we came to know later on when we became more familiar with the game. But we managed to play untiringly in that badminton court, thinking that we were then ready for the tournaments. Many new friends joined us in playing badminton in L D Engineering court. One was Anil Pandya and another was Dhananjay Rawal. Sometimes we were driven out of the badminton court by the students of L.D. Engineering or the caretaker of the badminton court. But we were shameless creatures and would again enter the badminton court illegally and play there until driven out.

One of us came with news one day that in Gandhinagar a state-level badminton tournament was going to be held. I, Anil and Dhananjay with the cousin of Dhananjay decided to participate in the tournament and actually participated. I could clear the first round of the tournament. Anil and Dhananjay could not clear even the first round of the tournament as they were not as good as I. My second match was scheduled in the evening. We three were exhausted after playing in the tournament. We had no food except a packet of Parle Biscuits. We bought bananas as none of us had enough money to eat a proper meal. We three ate biscuits and bananas. Sometime after eating, we got very thirsty. In those days, there was no concept of packaged water bottles. We, therefore, searched for water. We found a water cooler in the adjoining building near the badminton court. We got excited to see a water cooler. We reached the cooler and quenched our thirst by drinking water from the cooler tap. After drinking water while we were standing near the cooler, suddenly a big goat appeared. The goat reached the cooler tap and lifted up the tap nozzle with its mouth and started drinking water from the same water cooler. We were astonished by the sight. The style in which the goat was drinking water from the same cooler tap, we could discern that the goat was a regular visitor of the water cooler. We could not stop our laughter as we found ourselves drinking water from the same tap used by animals for drinking water. Equality between human beings and animals was coincidentally established. On this planet, we found ourselves no better than the goat who drank water from the same cooler. Recounting this episode, we still laugh, but we have now realised from life experiences that we human beings are worse than animals.

In the evening when the second round was announced, my other two friends were eager to watch me play a superstar game. Unfortunately, in the second round, I faced a tough player who defeated me with 15-0. It was a sheer debacle. We losers went home with gloomy faces and started dreaming of better performance in the next tournaments.

While I was studying in college, I was selected as the 2nd best player to represent my college in an inter-college badminton tournament. The first selected player to represent our college was Ashad Shah. He was a far better player than I. He was one year ahead in college. Because of his game, I was impressed by Ashad. He was six feet two inches tall and a well-built boy. He weighed 95 kg in college days whereas I was barely 50 kg. Because of badminton, we became bosom friends. After Ashad left the college, I reached the 1st position in badminton to represent my college. Because I was representing my college, I got an opportunity to attend a badminton coaching camp organised by Gujarat University. It was a one month coaching camp. The coach found good potential in me. He, therefore, made me the leader of the selected players taking coaching under him. I lacked leadership quality and hence one player, by his craft, snatched away the leadership from me in a subtle manner. I realised this thing only when he, at the end of the coaching period, proclaimed in front of all gathered for the closing ceremony that he had played the leadership role in coaching. This experience made me alert. It was a life lesson for me not to be meek when you are entrusted with leadership. But still, I have not improved on this leadership quality because of my inherent nature of not thrusting anything upon anyone. Leadership requires stern actions and imposing your ideology upon others for the larger benefit of all concerned. I lacked manipulation skills also to retain power and an imposing personality.

Next year, I also got an opportunity to attend the coaching camp held by Gujarat University. I became better in badminton after two coaching camps. I would play an excellent game during practice but would lose in tournaments. Losing in tournaments continued happening to me as I did not possess the tournament temperament and tenacity to withstand adversity. In one tournament, I was leading by 13-0 against my opponent but suddenly I lost my cool and faced defeat with 17-15. In a tournament held by Ahmedabad Municipal Corporation, I reached the semi-finals. The opponent was not that good, but still, I lost in the semi-final and had to be content with a Bronze Medal. This is the only medal I won during college days worth mentioning in this book.

Badminton is a very costly game. It was not possible for me to afford shuttlecocks. I found one player who was playing in the indoor badminton court of Polytechnic College. His name was TNC Vijayanand. His father was in government service, and he would get free shuttlecocks from the employer. The only difficulty was he would come to play at 8 p.m. after the office time of his father. Because the game would start at 8 p.m., I would reach home after 10 p.m. My father abhorred reaching home late. He scolded me many times that he did not want such a championship if it caused reaching home late at night. But because of the intoxication youthful energy, I would pay scant regard to such sermons given by my father. I was so incorrigible that my father washed his hands of me. I continued playing. Vijayanand was five to six years younger than me. He was a very good player, but because of my experience and age difference, he would usually lose against me in practice. After he became an adult, he became a seeded player of the State of Gujarat. In one tournament at Surat, it so happened that in the first round I had to face Vijayanand. I lost against him. I came back home on the next available train grumbling about the loss.

In those days I had no support from my family for playing badminton. Other players would use Yonex racquets whereas I could buy locally made racquet. My racquet would remain in the repairing shop for more repairs than with me. Guts would frequently cut from the edge because of the inferior quality of the product. I would use shorts made by me by cutting loose trousers. Others would wear expensive Proline sportswear in those days as Adidas, Puma and Nike had not entered India. I always wished I could afford costly Proline sportswear. Buying a Yonex racquet was a dream for me. My friend Ashad was coming from a rich family and possessed more than one Yonex racquets. I just asked him if he could give me a cover of a Yonex brand racquet, I would be happy. He obliged me by giving one badminton racquet cover of Yonex brand which was extra with him. I thereafter started putting my racquet of local brand in the cover of Yonex brand and flaunted in public as if I possessed a Yonex racquet. I was indeed delighted to have at least a cover of a Yonex brand. It was also a dream to have a tracksuit usually worn by a sports person. Sometimes I would borrow an extra-large size tracksuit from my friend Ashad and would wear it just to have a glimpse in the mirror of how I looked wearing a tracksuit.

After completing college, I did not play badminton for long. At the age of 31, I restarted playing badminton but now at Sun N Step Club after a gap of almost ten years. I hardly played there for one and a half years since the players at Sun N Step Club would play doubles, and I was fond of playing singles. In doubles, I would get stuck at one place on the badminton court and was unable to match my partner. I was short of the skill required for playing doubles. I, therefore, stopped playing at Sun N Step, but I made some friends there.

When I was 45, I started feeling fatigue and a loss of concentration. At that time coincidentally, a doctor client named Dr. Maulesh Shah came to me for his case. He was an orthopaedic surgeon, but I expressed to him my physical condition that I was feeling down, tired, and monotonous. He advised me that I should play any fast sports. At that time, I had just started playing volleyball in our society. The only difficulty in playing volleyball was that it would give bruises on my hand since my skin is wafer-thin. Sometimes it would injure my fingers or thumb too. So, I welcomed the suggestion of Dr. Maulesh and stopped playing volleyball and decided to start playing badminton again. I went to Sun N Step Club where some of the players were still playing badminton when I left badminton in the year 1996-97. They welcomed me with enthusiasm as my game was good. This time I made up my mind to get accustomed to playing doubles and accept it as the only option. I gradually improved my doubles game. I became quite proficient in doubles too. Now I am fully enjoying badminton doubles. Still, badminton singles are my favourite. Badminton gave me many friends and made my life full of exuberance. My badminton friends' range is very wide from a player aged 30 to a player aged 75. Those badminton friends who have made my life full of happiness are Vishnuprakash sir, Ashok Walia, Kamal Kumar Gosh, Abhay Damle, Vijay Chandorkar, Rajesh Amin, Manoj Somani, Pardeep Bhutoria, Manish Patel, Virat Popat, Nishith Gandhi, Samrendra Ganotra, Pratik Agarwal, Jignesh Ladwani, Suresh Panwar, Madanbhai, Yogesh Patel and his son Mohit Patel. These were the players with whom I had spent a considerable amount of time playing badminton and having parties. Mr. Vasu, who played with us, passed away two years ago. Many of the above players have shifted to other cities, but our bond is as good as it was before they moved out of Ahmedabad. There are other players who help us continue playing badminton when we are short of players, and one of them is Hardik Parikh who, despite being a champion, would play with us at the request of Vishnuprakash sir or any of us. Vishnuprakash sir is the main person who takes all efforts to keep us connected. Because of him, I am in contact with the past badminton players viz. Sushilbhai, Vijay Poddar, Saurabh Parikh with whom I had no opportunity to play badminton.

I have started playing in the State and National tournaments again after I attained the age of 50. In the Surat Gujarat state Veteran badminton Tournament, I reached the semi-finals and got an opportunity to qualify for the tournament to be played in Spain since the winner of the tournament was not keen to go to Spain. I had to defeat another semi-finalist to qualify to go to Spain, which I could not do. My dream to go to Spain got buried in my mind without its actual manifestation.

Be that as it may, I am keeping good health mainly because of badminton and my badminton friends. I wish to play badminton until I die and enjoy the friendship with my badminton friends throughout my life.

Chapter 8

First Experience of Intoxication and a Journey on the Train Roof

In the last year of my college or immediately after my graduation, I do not remember exactly, we friends decided to go to Mount Abu. None of us had any vehicle in those days; hence, it was decided to go to Mount Abu by train. We, eight friends, were Mehul Buddh, Mehul Sheth, Darshan Sheth, my brother Ashesh, my cousin Aashish, Mayur Majithia, and Rakshit Pandit. We booked tickets for the Agra Local, which would start at 11 P.M. at night and reach Abu Road at 6 A.M. The train would take seven hours to travel two hundred kilometres. Anyway, we reached Abu Road at six in the morning. From there, we took a state road transport bus to reach Mount Abu. It was my first tour with friends, and so it was for most of my other friends. We were very excited to explore our new world. We booked a dormitory in Gujarat Bhavan. The charge for the dormitory for ten persons was ninety-six rupees. Since we were only eight, it cost us Rs.12 each per day. We stayed for five to six days. None of us had ever had alcohol in life before. We had seen someone drinking alcohol in films/movies only. We all went to a liquor store. One of us purchased a beer bottle, one purchased a small whisky bottle, and one purchased a small gin bottle. We came back to our dormitory with the above stuff purchased from a liquor store. Nobody had any idea how to consume it. Like a film hero, we opened the whisky bottle and drank directly from the bottle. It was horrible. Then we drank beer from the bottle; God knows whether it was chilled or not. The taste of beer was also not good. Then we tried gin. Every one of us drank liquor from each other's bottle not knowing how to drink. My body was not accustomed to liquor consumption. By the evening, my body started showing signs of a reaction. It started with itching on every part of the body, and then the whole body became red like copper. The next day, it was unbearable. So, I consulted Dr. Raj Dhwan, who had a clinic in Mount Abu. He gave me an injection which cost me Rs.35. At the end of the tour, we each spent an average of Rs.200, whereas I spent Rs.235, which included the doctor's fee. The first experience of liquor consumption proved to be very costly for me. Still, my friends recount that episode and remind me that I became a Red Indian from Indian on that day!

While returning from Mount Abu, firstly we reached Abu Road Railway Station. The station was very crowded. The train that came first for Ahmedabad had no space to enter in any coach. We did not realise what to do. Two of us could, with great difficulty, enter the train coach. The rest of us were still on the railway platform. We suddenly saw that the crowd was climbing the train coaches and occupying the train roof. We followed the crowd, and we also occupied the roof of the train. The train started running, and it was simply an indescribable experience. Initially, we were scared, but very quickly we became comfortable on the train roof. We were sitting opposite to the wind direction so, whatever we ate would directly come to our mouth with the force of the wind. We still recount eating high-speed Chevada (a mix of namkeen) and laugh at it. There was a parallel system of serving tea, snacks, etc. on the roof of the train. One small boy would walk on the train roof with a tea kettle and sell it while the train is in motion. We were surprised to find the boy's dexterity to serve tea on the train roof during the running train. By the time the train reached Palanpur station, we became dark black being exposed to direct sunrays, the wind velocity, and coal dust emanating from the steam engine of the train. Our hair became like jute threads. We all got thirsty because of the constant exposure to the sun and wind for two hours. At Palanpur station, we ordered a cold drink from the roof of the train. The cold drink vendor was a little surprised to get an order from the train roof as the cold drink was considered to be expensive for common men. He first demanded money as he thought that we might not pay him, and the train would start. Apart from that, he did not trust us ruffians like youths having faces smeared with coal dust emanating from the steam engine, thinking that we would not be able to afford it. When we paid him money, he was happy to give us the cold drinks.

One of us said that in the future we would have a possibility to be on the platform of every station, but we would never be able to touch the roof of every station. So, we got excited to hear this suggestion. We therefore touched the roof of every station the train passed through. We came back home with great joy and satisfaction of having achieved an exceptional accomplishment of touching the roof of every station. I was slightly disappointed because I had to spend a huge amount of Rs. 35 on treatment for an allergy due to the consumption of liquor.

Chapter 9

Walk Alone, Walk Alone – Walking Became Part of My Life Without Choosing It

My walking experiences are numerous. From early childhood, I would walk to school. Every day, I walked four kilometres to reach the University Bus-stand to catch a bus for my school which was situated in Maninaga area. The same routine continued for three years. When I was six years old and studying at Bhakt Vallabh Dhola School, one day I walked from Shah e Alam bus stop to my home near Gujarat University just to save five paisa and buy a chocolate. When I got admission to Nutan School, I would walk an average of ten kilometres every day to reach the school located off Ashram Road. Upon getting admission to the municipal swimming pool near Stadium Six Roads, I would walk six to seven kilometres to reach the swimming pool as I did not have a bicycle.

In my father's view, my brother Ashesh and I were useless creatures. Good for nothing. He thought that during vacation time, his sons should at least learn the philosophies of Mahatma Gandhi, Vinoba Bhave, and Ravi Shankar Maharaj. He came to know that a National Youth Project's camp was to be held at Vasad under the guidance of one Mr. Subba Rao, who had done lots of social work in the Chambal area of Morena District of Madhya Pradesh. We were sent by our father to be part of that NYP camp. It was a camp for ten days. The objectives of the NYP camp were to inspire youths to do social services, to inculcate values such as hard work, truth, and concern for our fellow brothers and sisters, etc. The camp was in the midst of the gorges/ravines of River Mahi. It was a thrilling experience. There were no toilets, and we had to defecate in the natural surroundings amidst the chirping of birds and the breeze coming from the riverside. The camp was attended by more than one hundred and fifty youths from all states of India. There we did manual labour of digging pits with spades and shovels, planted trees, made walls of clay/bunds to prevent land erosion. Sometimes we were given work in the kitchen to cook food for all one hundred and fifty youths. Every day we were to attend the prayer in the morning, singing patriotic songs and regional songs. The last four days were a walk of ninety kilometres from Vasad to Ahmedabad. It was indeed a great experience. We started from Vasad and passed through Adas, Vadod, Anand, Lambhvel, Kanjari, Nadiad, Mehmdavad, Hathijan, Vatva, and reached Ahmedabad. Every day we were to walk twenty kilometres. At the end of the camp, we became better youths for some time but soon thereafter became as useless as we were before.

Thus, somehow walking became part of my life. One day after my college days while doing internship with R G Shah & Co, I went for an audit to Bombay with other senior audit staff. My friend Ashad, who had a house in Bombay, said that his cousin was fond of walking, and he would like to have company for a long walk. I was more than willing to go for a long walk. I met Ashad's cousin at 5 a.m. near Andheri Station. We started a morning walk from Andheri, walked for five hours, and reached Nariman Point, which is at a distance of twenty-five kilometres from Andheri. I still remember that useless twenty-five-kilometre walk just done for boasting and a laugh at it.

Similarly, just to show my strength and stamina, I boasted in front of my friends when we were in Mount Abu that I could walk from Mount Abu to Gurushikhar Point and come back on the same day. I asked my friends whether anyone was willing to be part of the walk. My friend Dhananjay was like me. He said he was ready to walk with me. We started at 8 a.m. and came back at 6 p.m., fully exhausted. We passed through small, neat, and clean villages of Mount Abu. We attended natural calls in the open at several points while walking from Mount Abu to Guru Shikhar and back. We thought our friends staying in Gujarat Bhavan would welcome us and praise our achievement. But they had decided something else for me and Dhananjay. As soon as we reached Gujarat Bhavan, one of our friends threw a blanket over our faces to ensure we could not find out who was beating us, and others started beating us playfully. My friend Dhananjay used the filthiest words for all who conspired to do the aforesaid act. In the evening, we decided to drink beer to relax and eat chicken. Somehow, after drinking beer and eating chicken, I started vomiting and got severe loose motions. It was a severe stomach infection. I went to the toilet eighteen times in one night and vomited four times. I would have died due to dehydration, but somehow, I did not die. I realised the futility of my boasting and taking the challenge of walking from Mount Abu to Gurushikhar and walking back to Mount Abu.

After joining the legal profession, walking remained a part of my life for one and a half years as I had no vehicle to reach the office or court. I still enjoy walking because it became a part of me without my choosing it.

Chapter 10

Aversion of Reading Books and Learning English Language

My father wanted that his children should cultivate the habit of reading at least Gujarati books, novels, magazines and newspapers. So, he would subscribe to magazines and special newspapers like Phoolwadi, Phantom, Navnit Samarpan, Akhandanand etc. meant for the overall development of children. However, despite my father's best efforts, I did not read anything. I must admit that I abhorred reading. I, therefore, avoided reading even newspapers until I reached the age of 22. I have, therefore, very little general knowledge of history, geography, science and politics. My father also wanted that we should learn good English. During our school days, we learnt the English language as one of the subjects of our syllabus only. I, my brother and sister studied in Gujarati medium throughout. I did my LL. B also in Gujarati medium. During my school days, my mother would teach me the English language from English Pathmala (Three or four volumes containing lessons for learning English grammar). Whatever little English we knew at that time, the credit goes to our mother. She essentially taught us English grammar and the syllabus books. Because of that my grammar is quite better than the grammar of many others. To see that his children learn good English, my father bought a book for spoken English from the British library in Ahmedabad. He also bought us one gramophone record player. In those days audio records containing listening material were known as LPs. The set of LPs contained the material printed in the book for improving spoken

English brought by my father from the British Library, Ahmedabad. The record player contained a button or indicator to adjust the speed of record playing as per the technical requirement of records. In those days records were available in three different speeds either the speed of 32 or 45 or 75 depending on the technical aspects of the originally recorded speed. Thus, the record had to be played according to the speed at which the original voice was recorded on it. My father was not a techno-savvy and so were we. He without reading the manual, thought that for the beginners of English the record was supposed to be played at the speed of 32, for middle-level students at the speed of 45 and for the higher level at the speed of 75. This belief of my father was not correct. We were also fools and had no interest in what our father did for us. We never looked at the technical specifications of the records bought by our father. I of late came to know that our records for spoken English were to be played at 45 speeds as originally recorded. My father started playing the first record at the speed of 32, which was the lowest. The result was the gramophone amplifier created a very hollow sound as if the sound was coming from a far distance. It would take one minute to complete one sentence. If it were played at the usual speed, the record would be over within 15 minutes, but when played at the speed of 32, it would take 45 minutes to complete the entire record. We got exhausted listening to the first record which lasted for 45 minutes instead of 15 minutes. Apart from the fact it consumed a long time, it was tough to bear the weird hollow sound. The net outcome was that we lost interest in learning spoken English. We had no patience to sit at one place for a long time and listen to the boring record. When we played the record at the speed of 75, it would create a sound of bickering of birds, and we would laugh at it. Somehow, we did not play it at the speed of 45 which was a correct speed. Anyway, we did not take English learning seriously through the gramophone record purchased from the

British library. Since I had learnt English as one of the subjects of my syllabus, my vocabulary was very poor. One day somebody asked me to say my initials, I was baffled by the question. I did not understand what do initials mean. When I was in the second year of college, somebody asked me about my residence address. I started gazing at him without following what he meant to convey. When I joined the legal profession, more particularly high court practice, neither did I possess good knowledge of English nor a good command of the Gujarati language. Knowledge of law was abysmally low. I tried to hide my lack of knowledge of the language by remaining silent most of the time. Our Senior would always recommend us not only read the judgements or law journals but to read other books as well. After having failed in the English language in LL. B 3rd year examination and after joining the legal profession, I took up the challenge to learn English very seriously. Somebody recommended that if anyone wanted to improve English, he must read newspapers loudly every day. One should also start doing conversations with friends in English. I followed the advice and started reading newspapers loudly. I made it a point to learn five new words every day so that my vocabulary is improved. Initially, I found it difficult to understand the titles of the news items forget the contents of the news item. I would find out five new words every day. Try to understand the word by looking into the dictionary. I would not only try to find out the meaning but its origin, pronunciation and other aspects so that I may not forget the new word I had learnt. I would also use the said word in two or three sentences so that it is permanently remembered by me in my mind. I continued this practice for about the initial five years and became a little comfortable in the English language.

My spoken English was also not as good as would be indicated in the later chapters. The advice of having conversations with friends in English usually resulted in silence as neither I nor my friends could form a full sentence. Even if I ventured to speak a sentence, I would fumble and stutter. Despite these initial difficulties, I started conversations in English with people who were equally weak like me in English. As mentioned earlier, I would fumble a lot, but gradually I gained the courage and competence to complete a sentence in English. I was still hesitant to stand up in court and argue a case in English. While arguing a case, I made many mistakes in the court proceedings. The fact that I was a Gujarati medium student and did not know the English language continued to linger in my mind for a considerable amount of time. I was hesitant while making arguments mainly because I thought that being a Gujarati medium student, I could never be fluent in spoken English, besides lacking knowledge of the law. It took me approximately 15 to 20 years to be confident in speaking the English language in public.

Anyway, now I cannot cling to the past and blame my studying in Gujarati medium as an excuse for not being at par with others since I have spent thirty-five years in the legal profession which is more than my twenty-one years of study in Gujarati medium. Now I can with confidence say that I may not be superior to many lawyers so far as the English language is concerned but at the same time, I am not inferior to them. Be that as it may, my whole English learning process was hilarious, full of using incorrect vocabulary.

Chapter 11

Purposeless Loitering During College Days

In 12th standard, ultimately, I got a reasonably good percentage to get admission to a reputed college named H. A. College of Commerce on my own merit. I had a choice of going to an arts college or to a commerce college. In our days, only girl students would choose the art faculty for further study. I had, therefore, no other option but to select the commerce faculty for my further study. If I had selected the arts stream, I had a fear of being branded as a girlish person. The commerce stream for college became my choice without any reason as the science stream was not my cup of tea.

In college days, usually all other friends would come on their individual scooters or in their cars. I had no vehicle. Therefore, I would use the bicycle which was given to me by my father to go to college. But I used to feel embarrassed to ride on a bicycle to go to college. I would, therefore, go to my friend Anil Pandya's home, and then if he had a scooter, we would ride on his scooter, which was most of the time not available. I and Anil, therefore, went on the same bicycle. I would pedal the bicycle, and he would ride the bicycle as a pillion. Since riding on a bicycle in the college campus would embarrass me, I and Anil would park my bicycle near the gate situated on the backside of the college where no one could notice us. We would thereafter enter from the back door with good clothing in style. My college days had nothing great to be mentioned in this book. It was just purposeless loitering with friends, fun, and frolic. We would enjoy friendships, eat something and go for movies or to a friend's house to pass our time. I would like to name a few of my college friends. They were and are Ashad Shah, Anil Pandya, Dhananjay Raval, Darshan Sheth, Amish Shah, Paresh Panchal, Bhadresh Shah, Saurang Shah, Viren Choksi, and Sameer Udeshi. Since I was very shy, I did not have any girlfriend. Because of my badminton craze, my badminton partner Ashad became my best friend. I started visiting his home occasionally and met his family. I was impressed by the liberal way of living in his family. I started going to his home regularly and became part of his family in no time. His family had a great interest in art, music, and dance. Ashad's brother Maulik is a great dancer, and he was pursuing dance in Kadam Institute of Kathak Dance. He also became my very close friend. Through them, I met Ashit Sanghavi who had then come from Bombay to Ahmedabad for doing business in Shares and Stocks. I have many fond memories with Ashad, Maulik, and Ashit. I have spent the best time of my life with them. Because of my association with the family of Ashad and Maulik, I became interested in music.

In those days I did not have good clothes. I would therefore borrow clothes from my friends whenever I was to attend any marriage or other important functions. I was roaming aimlessly, and I had no inclination for earning, or I may say I had no capacity to earn. I had no goals in my life. One day I was wearing very good clothes and asked my friend Ashit Sanghvi about my new clothes. He did not respond well and sarcastically said, "You must have borrowed the new clothes I was wearing from Ashad or Maulik." A couple of times he ridiculed me, saying that I was a parasite in the home of Ashad and Maulik. Those taunts brought a late realisation to my mind that it was time to take life seriously. I am therefore grateful to Ashit Sanghavi for his taunts that made me a little responsible and to Ashad-Maulik for making me part of their family where I found lots of love and care.

Chapter 12

Music Madness Fizzled Out

My music madness continued for approximately three four years. After becoming part of Ashad-Maulik's family as stated earlier, I got fascinated by music, more particularly Hindustani Classical Music. I decided to learn the *Tabla*. I initially joined Saptak School of Music. I learnt the *Tabla* there for two to three months, which was not an enriching experience. In the meantime, I was told by my sister Nandini's friend Roopa Mehta that her uncle was in the field of teaching *Tabla*. So, I contacted Shri Umeshbhai Mehta, the uncle of Roopa, for learning *Tabla*. My *Tabla* training started. In my family, there was no great love for music. From my childhood, I had no exposure to music except listening to only two programmes of music broadcast on Akashvani Radio i.e. Gujarati *Geeto no Karyakram* "*Geet Saurabh*" and *Sangit Sarita* (a programme of Hindi film songs based on *Raag* and a short introduction of *Raag*). Barring these programmes, my father did not permit us to listen to any other music. My sister would listen to the *Sangit Sarita* programme, but I was not interested in it. I, therefore, lacked a basic sense of music. I did not know anything about *Taals* (rhythmic cycles) or beats. I came to know for the first time that the first beat of any Taal is called the "sum". The words *Kayda, Palta, Tukda, Paran, Tihai, Chakradhar Tihai, Peshkar, Theka, Laggi* associated with *Tabla* playing were completely foreign to me. I overcame the initial difficulties of learning *Tabla* in six months. After six months, I bought a pair of *Tabla*. I started doing *Riyaz* (practice) for four to five hours a day. In one or two years, my fingers on the *Tabla* started moving swiftly, but my mind was unable to grasp the finer nuances of *Tabla* playing. I would, therefore, play the basic *Theka* (rhythmic cycle) without value addition, any variation, or innovation. Because of my keen interest in Tabla, I was looking for opportunities to do *Tabla* accompaniment with any vocalist or an instrument player. Due to my friendship with Maulik Shah, a renowned Kathak dancer, I got to meet Rameshbhai Bapodara, an accomplished *Tabla* player. I started getting guidance from him too. I became his family member too. He would teach me *Tabla*, and I would look after his daughter Tanya and would go to drop Tanya at her school on the moped provided by him for that specific purpose. His wife, Manjariben, also treated me like her brother. Rameshbhai Bapodara introduced me to one vocalist, Shirishbhai Pandit. He was also looking for a free *Tabla* accompanist. Shirishbhai and I decided to sit for Riyaz. He would sing Hindustani Classical, and I would try to accompany him on Tabla. In a short time, I could manage playing a *Vilambit Theka* (rhythm at a slow pace), which is considered to be a difficult job. It requires constant counting of beats in the mind while playing *Tabla*. Madhya Laya (moderate pace) was not difficult for me. The fastest Laya (pace) was not the need of vocal singing. I would go to his home on my bicycle with the pair of *Tabla* and would play the *Tabla* as an accompaniment. I met one Sohanbhai Nilkanth, a Sarod player, and arranged accompaniment with him also. For doing accompaniment with Sarod, one would require to play *Tabla* with great speed known as Dhrut Laya. I could manage the Dhrut Laya also with Sohanbhai, but as said earlier, my fingers started moving swiftly on the *Tabla*, but my mind could not introduce new variations or innovations. As a result, my *Tabla* playing became monotonous and mechanical. I was unable to find time to introduce variations between two beats or understand different variations of the same *Theka* or coming back to the "sum" (the first beat of the rhythmic cycle) with different variations. I started playing the *Tabla* in small family functions. In those days, I considered Hindi film music to be inferior and never tried to focus on *Tabla* playing with Hindi songs. Off late, I realised that playing *Tabla* with classical vocal or instrument in public stage shows was not my cup of tea. In all those functions where I got opportunities to play *Tabla*, I could not impress anyone with my *Tabla* skill. In fact, I was not impressed by myself. In the society where I was staying with my parents, one of the neighbours, Himmatbhai, used to sing devotional Jain music in *Derasars* (Jain Temples). He invited me to play *Tabla* with him in *Derasar*. He knew that I was a novice, so he kept one professional *Tabla* player with him to do accompaniment. The professional Tabla player told me to follow his *Tabla* playing during the devotional singing. I could not manage following him as I used to listen to classical music, and I had no idea how to play certain *Thekas* or the pattern of *Thekas* that are usually being played in devotional and filmy music. My experience of *Tabla* playing in the *Derasar* was really terrible. I realised that I was not fit to play the *Tabla* with light music. I disliked the people who ushered us into the *Derasar* addressing us *Gavaiyaas* (lower-class singers) and *Tabla as Dholkas*. I gave an excuse to myself for the poor show in *Derasars* that I was skilled to play Hindustani Classical Music and not light devotional music to be performed in *Derasars*.

I gradually became more and more passionate about classical music. I religiously attended the annual Saptak Festival of Music for more than fifteen years on my bicycle. At 3.30 a.m. on winter nights, I would return home from the Saptak Festival on my bicycle with the same enthusiasm. I would attend any classical music programme in Ahmedabad, whether I was invited or not. I attended one such private programme of Flute by Pandit Hariprasad Chaurasia and *Tabla* by Ustad Zakir Hussain at the home of the well-known industrialist Mr. Chintan Parikh near *Gulbai Tekra* without an invitation. I not only attended the programme but also had dinner there without an invitation. In this programme, I saw

Ustad Zakir Hussain, a *Tabla* wizard, perform for the first time and was mesmerised by his personality and performance. After listening to Zakir Hussain, he became my idol. I still believe that I have never heard a *Tabla* player as good as him. There are many such instances of attending wedding programmes where the maestros of Indian Classical music performed, and I attended such wedding functions without an invitation and ate dinners that followed the functions.

Because of my friend Maulik, I came to know Niraj Parikh (now Pandit Niraj Parikh), an accomplished vocalist. I expressed my wish to do *Tabla sangat* (accompaniment) with him. He was happy that I was willing to do practice sessions with him without charging any amount. In fact, I was an amateur *Tabla* player and therefore could not dream of asking any amount from him. It was actually an opportunity and an honour for me to do practice with Niraj Parikh and his father, Pandit Krishnakant Parikh. I got a couple of opportunities to do *Tabla* sangat with Niraj and his father in private *Bethaks* (small-scale private functions). But deep down, I was not happy as I was not able to do variations like a professional *Tabla* player during *Tabla* sangat with Pandit Niraj Parikh and Pandit Krishnakant Parikh. Nevertheless, I kept on doing Sangat with them occasionally until I joined the legal profession.

One day Pandit Shirishbhai gave me an exciting news that I had to do *Tabla* sangat with him in a large-scale stage show organised by Ustad Kadarkhan's Music School Naad Niket. It was a stage show of renowned artists from Ahmedabad city. I and Shirishbhai started doing rigorous Riyaz. I memorised a few *Tihais* to use them in the beginning of the performance. The invitation cards of the programme were distributed to all music lovers. Unfortunately, the fiasco started with the printing of my name in the invitation card. The invitation cards mentioned my name as "Asim Bhatt" instead of Asim Pandya.

I thought of the famous quote "what is there in a name" and brushed aside the pain of incorrect printing of my name in the invitation cards. On the programme day, we were ready to ignite the stage. Since it was my first public show, my friends, relatives, and even my father came to watch us performing on the stage. All of them showered their best wishes. Some friends came with a bouquet of flowers. They all occupied their seats in the auditorium not knowing what was going to be unfolded in a short time. The duration of the programme was three hours, but Naad Niket Music School had invited more than six artists to perform. The first performance of someone lasted for more than forty-five minutes. The second performance also lasted beyond the time given to the artist. By the time the third performance was to begin, all remaining artists lost their patience. They thought that they would not get a chance to perform. The artists went crazy to occupy the stage. The artists started rushing onto the stage as soon as one artist finished his performance. Whether his name was announced as the next performer or not, he would rush to the stage and put his harmonium or *Tabla* to secure his performance. I and Shirishbhai both were not smart. We simply kept waiting for our names to be announced by the anchor. The auditorium was booked up to 12 hours of that night as per the rules of the auditorium. Finally, at 12 hours, the curtain fell, and the auditorium was shut down by the management of the auditorium. We did not get a chance to perform in our first stage show. It was a total fiasco. My family members, friends, and relatives went back home disappointed and dejected as they missed the chance to see me performing on the stage. I and Shirishbhai went to his home. We had tea and snacks at his home. We laughed at the total debacle of our stage show. I am unable to forget this memorable stage show even after the efflux of almost thirty-five years after that event.

During one Saptak Music Festival, I got an opportunity to watch Pandit Samta Prasad performing *Tabla* solo. He played for two hours, and I became his fan. He was from Banaras. I decided to be his disciple in Banaras. I started correspondence with him through post. In those days, the post was the only medium of communication. He was kind to give a reply, and he said he would teach me *Tabla* without knowing my ability. He might have thought that I was an advanced student, which I was not. The correspondence between me and him continued for about six months. Finally, I realised that if I went to learn *Tabla* at the age of 22 in Banaras, I would not be able to earn for at least the next ten years. Moreover, I had no money to sustain myself without earning for the next ten years. Wisdom prevailed, and I gave up the idea of learning *Tabla* from Pandit Samta Prasad.

After passing through the period of three to four years of music madness, the wisdom dawned upon me that it was not a good decision to start my career in *Tabla* at the age of 22. I was therefore constrained to think of other options. My euphoria for music evaporated, but my love for music has still remained intact.

Chapter 13

A Strange Decision to Bring a Child in the First Year of Marriage

During college days, I did not have any girlfriend. I think that I did not possess that charm a girl expects from a boy. I was sceptical whether I would ever get a bride or not. My other friends got married, and I was the only one left out. My friend Anil Pandya was also like me. He was also from a middle-class background and had failed to make a girlfriend during college days. Finally, his destiny changed, and he got married. After the marriage of Anil, I felt that I too have a chance to get a bride. My lost hopes got revived. In the year 1991, while I was pursuing LL.M after joining the profession of law, I got news from my maternal aunt that someone known to her was looking for a boy for her niece's marriage. I was a little surprised to find the proposal for my marriage. I asked my mother and my cousin Aashish to have a first meeting with the girl without my presence. I told them if they find the girl suitable for me, I would meet her. My mother and Aashish met the girl named Ragini Joshi who had come from Delhi to find a prospective groom. They had an informal conversation with the girl and found her suitable for me and suggested to me that I could go ahead with the proposal. On the next day, Ragini and I met at my home. That was my first experience of life to have met a girl for the purpose of marriage. I did not think much about my future, and in the first meeting, I asked Ragini whether she found anything worth in me to proceed with the marriage. She said yes, and from my end, it was an obvious yes as I thought why should I explore more options when the girl I met was decent. Our parents fixed the betrothal. The engagement was done on 21/2/1991. After my engagement with Ragini, we communicated through letters for a period of nine months as she was residing in Delhi, and she had no facility of a landline phone in her home. In those days, we occasionally communicated through STD phones. I wrote letters in the English language to impress Ragini, and she was also impressed. God knows what kind of English I must have written! The second reason for writing letters in English was to improve my English as I was facing troubles in communicating in English during my profession. Ragini has preserved all letters, but I have no courage to read them again for the reason that the letters must be containing ludicrous English. Finally, we got married on 23/11/1991.

During my college days, I felt that my parents committed a mistake in bringing me into the world at the age of forty. By the time I turned 18, they retired from service. I, therefore, did not get the opportunity to explore various career options. At the age of 18, it became a burden for me to think of earning without trying different experiments that I was fond of. I believed that I could not make a career in music because of the responsibility to start earning thrust upon me by circumstances. I, therefore, decided that I would not delay bringing a child after my marriage. After two months of my marriage, when Ragini did not conceive, I got worried. We went to our family doctor and expressed our concern. Our family doctor was surprised to know my concern. He said I must keep patience and suggested that it would happen naturally. He said that if there was a long passage of time after marriage and if my wife did not conceive, I should consult him again. Very soon thereafter, somewhere in February 1992, we got news that Ragini was pregnant. We were excited to hear this news. Before our first marriage anniversary, we had a baby girl in our life. On our first marriage anniversary, we clicked a photo with our beloved daughter in our hands. We were very happy and thrilled to have a child in the first year of marriage. We gave the name "Shaivaa" to our daughter.

Chapter 14

Overcoming the Health Issue of Our Daughter

Our daughter was brought up absolutely normally until the age of six. At the age of six, we came to know that she had a small internal deformity in her spine. My wife and I became very sad and started worrying about Shaivaa's health. We met expert spine doctors in Ahmedabad, Bombay, Delhi, and Bangalore. All doctors advised spine surgery considering the nature of the deformity's development. In those days, I did not have enough money to get the surgery done in Bombay. We had Mediclaim for her, but it was not cashless. So, my father, my brother, and I jointly collected the necessary funds for Shaivaa's surgery in Bombay. You would be surprised to note that the cost of surgery was Rs. 80,000 (eighty thousand) only. But I did not even have that small amount. The surgeon said he would perform a smaller surgery instead of opening the whole spine. If that small surgery arrested the growth of the deformity, it would be best. The surgery, which lasted for three to four hours, was done. Ten days later, we came back home. We were asked to do regular follow-ups and keep an eye on the growth of the deformity. After returning from Bombay, I forwarded my Mediclaim to the insurance company for reimbursement. Unfortunately, the insurance company refused to reimburse the amount spent on the surgery. I was completely shattered but decided to fight. I filed a complaint in the consumer forum. I could have had the case decided in my favour by telling the presiding officer of the Consumer Forum that it was my personal case. The terms and conditions of the insurance policy were absolutely against us. It excluded pre-existing diseases and congenital external deformities from the insured risk. But I decided to fight the case on its own merit. I invoked many important legal principles during the arguments, such as *generalia specialibus non-derogant, contra proferentem*, etc. I asked the consumer court to interpret the exclusion clause of the insurance policy narrowly to exclude only those congenital deformities that were either known to the person or were visible. It would not exclude the internal deformity not known to us. After valiant efforts, I won the case, but the trouble did not end there. The insurance company filed an appeal before the Consumer National Commission. The National Commission, after hearing me and the insurance company, dismissed the appeal of the insurance company. I got the reimbursement of the amount spent on surgery after two to three years with interest. I gave back the amount borrowed from my father and brother to them from the claim amount received from the insurance company. I was satisfied with the outcome of the case and felt relaxed. But my state of relaxation did not last long.

Unfortunately, the operation could not arrest the growth of the deformity. Her spine started bending on one side creating a kind of scoliosis. After four years, the doctors advised a second surgery. My wife and I again got shattered by the thoughts of a second surgery. This time the doctors were to open the whole spine, fuse the thoracic portion of the spine, and place an Errington rod and wires inside. The operation started. Hours passed, but there was no news from the operation theatre. After six hours, still there was no communication from the operation theatre. We started crying, thinking that something must have gone wrong but still kept our hopes alive. After eight hours, the doctors came out from the operation theatre perspiring and in sweat-soaked clothes. The doctor said that the operation was successful. We again cried out of ecstasy, being relieved from tension. A sigh of relief was visible on our faces that our beloved daughter survived the surgery that lasted eight hours. After the surgery, the question of reimbursement of the expenses made on the surgery arose. But this time, my insurance claim was honoured because of the previous decision of the Consumer court. My wife and I were worried about the future of our daughter because of two major surgeries of the spine. She was advised to wear a specially made brace to support her spine. She was also asked to wear shoes of a special type, one shoe having a bigger sole to correct the leg discrepancy arising from the deformity. Our daughter Shaivaa got annoyed with these unusual things to be put on by her. One day, she declared that she would throw away both these unusual things as they constantly reminded her of her problem and actually did throw away those things. She started believing herself absolutely normal. She groomed herself in such a way that nobody could notice her physical problem. She participated in the "Clean Clear Fresh Face" contest and stood runner-up when she was in college. She participated in the Miss Ahmedabad Contest and won the title. She always projects herself beautifully and with elegance that we have also forgotten that she ever had any physical issue. In the year 2014, my daughter expressed her wish to study in the USA after completing her graduation in arts. Usually, students who study Engineering or Medicine think of studying in the USA as they are offered jobs after their study in the USA. My wife, Ragini, and I told Shaivaa that it would be difficult to find a university in the USA where she could pursue her further study. But she found one in New York and started the procedure for admission. She got admission, but the fee was enormous, 70,000 USD. In addition, I was supposed to make arrangements for her stay and food that might cost me 1,500 USD every month. I did not have enough money, so I mortgaged my home and obtained an educational loan as Ragini was keen to send her to the USA. If a student chooses not to stay in the college hostel known as dorms, she needed to give the name of a person willing to be her guardian, and the guardian should be a resident of New York. Staying in the dorms was very costly. So, we searched for a person staying in New York who would be willing to become her guardian. I had some impression that my father's friend's son named Sunil Bhatt was a resident of New York. I had never talked to him in the past and had never had the opportunity to meet him. But we thought of at least giving him a call and ask him whether he was willing to be the guardian of Shaivaa. I called him and explained my problem. He was very warm, and he readily said yes. I think I have never met a person like Sunil Bhatt in my life who is so enthusiastic and warm in maintaining relationships. His warm response to our proposal gave us great respite.

I knew that this investment was not going to get her a job in the USA but just to fulfil Shaivaa's dream, we decided to incur the expenditure on her higher education. It was a pure gamble. But as said earlier, adventurism, or you may say misadventurism, is in our DNA so we sent her to the USA. Shaivaa is also like me. She chose the less trodden path rather than joining me in my profession of law. She went to the USA in the year 2014 and studied there facing many difficulties up to 2017. As predicted, the USA government did not accept her H1b VISA though her name was picked up in the lottery. Finally, she had to come back to India, but I must say that my investment in her education did not go to waste. After her marriage when she went to Australia with her husband, she got a good job immediately because of her education in the USA.

My wife and I are proud of her for her courage in taking the deformity nonchalantly as if she is absolutely normal. We were worried about her marriage because of her spine issue, but everything went smoothly and normally. As mentioned earlier, she settled in Australia with her husband after their marriage and now trying to settle in Dubai by establishing her own business.

─◦◦◦─

Part-II

─◦◦◦─

My Unplanned Journey in Law Profession

Chapter 1

Failing in Law Examinations

After graduation, I was wondering and thinking about what to do. Based on my B. Com degree, it was not possible to get employment except in the field of marketing or accounts. I was a misfit for marketing as I lacked confidence and good communication skills. Therefore, I joined the law course to avoid the stigma of being branded as unemployed. I also simultaneously joined the Chartered Accountancy course just to flaunt in society that I was doing CA. In fact, I was not interested in either. My father, through his contacts, arranged my internship in the well-known firm R G Shah & Co. I started attending the aforementioned firm as an intern, but deep down, I was unhappy with the new discipline and the curtailment of my freedom. I started receiving a stipend of Rs. 15 every month, which was less than my expenses for reaching the office or audit places by bus. I was not aspiring to become a chartered accountant at all; it was just a pastime for me. The second reason for joining CA was so that my parents could say that their son was not unemployed but doing CA. My father spent Rs. 1500 and ordered reading material for CA, which I never opened or read. I was going for audits only for the purpose of enjoying snacks or lunch offered at the audit places. Except snacks, tea/coffee, and sometimes lunch, there was no other incentive for me to go to audit places. One day, I was made part of the audit team of four persons which was to go to Vadodara for an audit. We were provided accommodation in one guest house which was shabby. We had no option but to stay in that guest house. In the evening, one of us dared to propose to the other members of the audit team to go to a newly opened five-star hotel in the Alkapuri area in Vadodara for dinner. The other two reluctantly agreed to go to the five-star hotel for dinner even though it would cost us a lot. I was the junior most in the audit team, and hence I had no say in the aforementioned discussion. In fact, my existence in the audit team was insignificant. We finally decided to go and indeed ventured to enter with fear and hesitancy in the Five-Star Hotel of Welcome Group for dinner. We did not know what to eat in the five-star hotel as there were many varieties of food priced highly. One of us placed the order for food as per his own understanding of the menu. The waiter noticed that we were not people belonging to the five-star culture. We ordered three dishes for the four of us, which included roti too. The waiter looked at us with disdain and said that it would not be sufficient for the four of us and left us in embarrassment. We left it to the waiter to decide what food to bring and in what quantity! We finished dinner with half-empty stomachs and came out of the hotel thrilled to have had dinner in a five-star hotel. I got an opportunity to go to Bombay for an audit. It was my first experience of travelling in an AC coach of a train to Bombay. I had no prior experience of air-conditioned coach. Fearing the cool ambience of an AC coach, I kept warm clothes ready with me. I clad myself with warm clothes and a woollen cap as soon as I entered the AC coach. The passengers travelling with me were looking at me scornfully as I was overly dressed in warm clothes. But it was a nice experience of travelling in an AC coach for the first time. We stayed at the Sea Green hotel on Nariman Point, and I enjoyed the thrill of being in Bombay for one week.

But very soon after returning from Bombay, I got bored with doing an audit of accounts. It was a monotonous job of going to an audit place with a green pencil and putting tick marks in the account books.

I did not understand anything. Finally, I mustered enough courage to declare before my father that I did not want to do CA. I gave up CA within one and a half years. I did not even dare to attempt any examination.

Now, left with no other choice, I continued pursuing law without interest. I did not attend classes in law school. The Principal of Sir L A Shah Law College called me a couple of times and asked me to attend the classes regularly. But I was an obstinate fool. I did not pay attention to the advice of the principal. Since I was fully engrossed in leisure, I chose not to attend the classes. In those days, I do not know whether moot court and internship options were available or not. Be that as it may, I was not aware of such things. I never thought of availing a court exposure while pursuing law. As a result of this, I failed twice in LL.B. Once I failed in the subject "English for Lawyers," and I do not remember the subject where I failed the second time. But two half marksheets still bear testimony to my failing in LL.B. twice. The reason for failing was that I was more interested in making a career in music. As said earlier, I was passionate about music. After some time, I had a late realisation that I was not even fit for the Tabla. I did LL.B. in Gujarati medium reading mainly Parikh & Jhala publications of summaries of each subject and occasionally law books with commentary of Jhabvala's publications. In those days, it was believed that only studious students of Gujarati medium would read Jhabvala's publications of commentary. I was not studious at all, and hence Jhabvala was not my first option. I was not competent to write and speak the English language, and hence law books in English were obviously beyond my comprehension.

At last, I passed the LL.B. exam and became an advocate in the year 1989, not with flying colours but faded colours with two half mark sheets! Fortunately, in those days, there was no law stating that if a person had failed in a law course, they would not be entitled to practice law. Otherwise, I would have been doing some menial job at the mercy of a relative or a friend, as I was sure that on merit there was no scope for me to get decent employment with a high salary.

Chapter 2

◆◆

Jumping into Law Profession without Doing Groundwork

Finally, left with no other alternative for earning, I reluctantly joined law practice. I got a practice licence on 10th March 1989.

I got an advocate's coat stitched in the shop of one B. Durgaiya Tailor situated in Ratan Pol, the old city area of Ahmedabad. My cousin Ashish took me to that shop. I was told by the tailor that all high court judges get their black coats stitched in his shop. I was impressed by his boasting. This was my first experience in life of getting stitched a coat. When I put on the advocate's coat for the first time, it gave me feelings as if I had conquered the world I thought that I was fully ready for handling court cases and to appear in court unmindful of the fact that getting a law degree was one thing and to practice law was altogether a different game. My world was small, and I thought that a person becomes an advocate once he wears a black coat after passing LL.B exam. I had no idea of what kind of knowledge of law and language was needed to do law practice successfully. I was neither equipped with the knowledge of law nor having command of the English language. But, by the time I realised my incompetence in law and the language of the court, I had already embarked upon an unprepared journey in the profession of law. It was a *cul-de-sac* for me as there was no possibility to return to any other field for the want of any other qualification or skill.

Chapter 3

Feeling of Suffocation in the First Law Office

After joining the profession, I was wondering what to do and how to begin law practice. Someone advised me to practice in the trial court first and understand the law practice and basic procedure of the trial court. I thought it to be a good suggestion. I was advised to join the office of any well-established advocate in the city civil court, but I had no means to reach any. Several names were suggested to me upon inquiry from my small legal circle. I was strongly recommended to join one advocate who was considered to be the best civil side lawyer in Ahmedabad City Civil Court. I expressed my wish to join that advocate's office to my cousin Aashish, who had by that time joined the law profession for more than three years. He spoke to his father, who was a high court judge at that time, to recommend my name to the aforesaid advocate. My uncle in turn requested the late Justice Mr. K G Shah, who was the Principal City Civil and Sessions judge at that time, to ask the said advocate to accommodate me in his office. Finally, I could approach the said advocate through the recommendation of my uncle (masa) late Justice Mr. J P Desai and late Justice Mr. K. G Shah. I was asked to visit his office the next day. I, with great hopes and enthusiasm, went to his office wearing the best clothes available to me. I was made to sit outside the chamber of the aforesaid advocate for thirty minutes. Finally, the office bell rang from his chamber, and I was called by the advocate into his chamber. The clerk of the advocate ushered me into his chamber. The advocate stared at me from his reading glasses for one minute, looked at my untidy clothes and improperly combed hair. He with his experienced eyes gauged my potential in just one minute. He asked me a couple of questions for formality as he appeared to be least interested in me. The first question was about the medium of my study. I said "Gujarati". He bluntly said that he would not take an intern or a junior who had studied in Gujarati medium. To him, Gujarati medium students were incompetent to handle complex legal cases as all laws are enacted in English and all law journals report Supreme Court and high court cases in the English language. He said that in his office all pleadings were made in the English language and that I should first equip myself with good English. After this brief interaction, he clearly told me not to expect even a stipend from him as it was not his practice to pay anything to his juniors. My first meeting with the aforesaid advocate was disheartening as it belied my expectation of getting a stipend or salary, but I took solace that at least I got an opportunity to work under one of the best lawyers of the Ahmedabad City Civil Court. After joining his office just in a few days, I realised that my value in the office was less than the peon. I thought he valued his furniture more than me. He had such a personality that there was no scope for any interaction with him. He would maintain distance from his juniors. This was my perception of his personality and not the truth. I did not get any guidance from him or his other juniors to read or prepare a particular case in a particular manner. In his office, there were two other junior lawyers. They both were very able lawyers. They were good at understanding law, the English language, and expression. Later on, one became a Senior Advocate in the High Court of Gujarat, and another became a city court judge. I guess they also perhaps thought that I was a useless person having no knowledge of law or language. I had no courage to talk to them, and they both were a little introverted. Therefore, barring passing a smile occasionally, they did not interact with me. I remained on a silent mode for all time in the office of my aforesaid senior. I could not understand the procedure of civil litigation in the city civil court. The law jargons like notice of motion, summary suit, summons for judgement, leave to defend, chamber judge, auxiliary court, injunction application, attachment before judgement, Purshis, etc., were absolutely foreign to me. The abbreviations viz. SJ (Summons for Judgement), LD (leave to defend), NM (notice of motion), WS (written statement) would further confound my little brain. I was at a complete loss to understand anything. I, therefore, did not find the atmosphere in the city court congenial. I lost interest in law, more particularly city court practice, in a couple of months. In the period of six months, I hardly saw a full-fledged civil trial going on. Advocates would rush to different courts situated in the city court campus at 11 a.m., give adjournment applications, and by 11.30, they would be found in the advocates' club known as Gujarat Club leisurely having tea and snacks. I could not understand the nature of law practice. Juniors like me were not even allowed to enter the Gujarat Club. Nobody would even pass a smile at me. I did not find advocates in that court warm or friendly. Fed up with the suffocating environment of the city court and the office of my senior, I decided to escape from his office by any means. One day I mustered the courage to speak to him about my intention of not continuing his office. I said that I intended to do a masters in law and therefore was unable to continue his office. My senior perhaps knew that I was giving a false reason, but he welcomed my proposal to discontinue his office. I finally escaped from the office of my senior under the pretext of doing LL.M. I was relieved from the suffocating environment of the office of my senior. My senior was relieved much more than I as he could get rid of me, an unwanted beginner thrust upon him by the Principal City Civil judge late Mr. K. G Shah. My short journey in the city court ended in despair.

Chapter 4

Unceremonious Expulsion From My Senior's Office

After giving up city civil court practice in a short span of less than six months, I realised for the first time that now there was no option for me but to take up the legal profession sincerely even though it did not engender interest in my mind or heart. Though I had no knowledge of spoken or written English or law, by fortuitous circumstance I got an opportunity to join the office of Mr. K G Vakharia in the year 1989 upon the recommendation of my father. My father knew him well and since it was my father's request, Mr. Vakharia agreed to accept me as his junior. My father was a learnt man and a very respectable person. My father was a political analyst and reformist. He was a known name in Gujarati literature. So, Mr. Vakharia might have had a misconception that I too would at least have some knowledge of language and law. When I joined his office, there were six juniors attached to Mr. Vakharia. They were Mr. Jayant Patel (who became a high court judge later on), Mr. Ghanshyam Udhawani (who also became a high court judge later on), Mr. Percy Kavina (who became a Senior Advocate later on), advocate Mukesh Ambalal Patel, advocate Bindu Vakharia, and advocate Amee Magiawala. I was the seventh and the last in the row. Fortunately, because there were six juniors attached to Mr. Vakharia prior to my joining, my lack of knowledge of law and language did not get exposed to him. I was simply loitering in court with Bindu and Amee, the most junior colleagues, as I had not developed rapport with my other colleagues. Gradually, I started developing rapport with Ghanshyam Udhawani and Percy. Ghanshyam at least found me a good person and started mentoring me. He was in the good books of our senior. We were always told by our senior that we must emulate Ghanshyam for his hard work and dedication. Ghanshyam was also from a lower middle-class family, so we started getting along well.

After joining the high court practice, I did not get an opportunity to speak a single sentence in court for more than one year. After about fourteen months of my joining law practice, a day came when I spoke my first sentence in court in the English language before justice N B Patel: "Mylord, please keep back the matter." I came out of the courtroom cheerfully as if I had won the case as it was my first court utterance in law practice. In those days of my initial practice, Ghanshyam was my idol in the office. In most of the cases of Mr. Vakharia, the advocate on record would be invariably Ghanshyam. As said earlier, he was very sincere and hardworking. I gradually developed a friendship with him, and we became very good friends. I was impressed by Percy's English and his oratory, but it took time to develop a friendship with him. He also became my dear friend later on. Since I had very little knowledge of the English language, I selected Mukesh Ambalal Patel to start a conversation with him in English as I thought he was like me in the matter of the knowledge of law, language, and expression. We both were from a lower-middle-class family and lacked financial means to sustain in the profession. I was staying in Professors' Colony, Near Vijay Cross Roads, and Mukesh would come from Vastrapur area on a city bus. He was staying in Lake View Apartments, made for a middle-income group of society. He would get down at Vijay Cross Roads Bus Stop from the bus. He would reach our senior's office near Navarang School, Naranpura, on foot. I also did not have a vehicle, so I would also walk to the office every day. Sometimes we would walk together to reach the office if coincidentally we meet. But while returning from the office, Mukesh and I would invariably walk together. We both knew that we were poor in the English language. We, therefore, decided to at least speak with each other in English. We mutually agreed to start a conversation in broken English while walking back home from the office. Sometimes due to a lack of expression power in English, we would walk silently as we were not in a position to form a sentence. The correlation of thoughts and speech was not happening for the want of sufficient vocabulary and the sentence construction skill. After the passage of about eight months and some practice, we could manage a conversation in English with slight confidence. I do not know about Mukesh, but for me, it was a great victory over my handicap. Now, to some extent, I was ready for advocacy as I had gathered a little knowledge of law and language in about more than one year of practice.

To my utter surprise, one day I got my first case through a reference of my father after one and a half years of law practice in the high court. It was a service matter of an employee engaged for 29 days of service every month with an artificial break of one day. To my good luck, such a practice was not approved by many judicial pronouncements. I drafted the petition with the help of my father. I prepared the case well and took out those decisions of the High Court of Gujarat on the same issue for presenting it before the court. The petition was listed before Hon'ble Justice B. S Kapadia. I was told by some junior lawyers that I should, before the opening of the case, tell the court that this was my maiden appearance. When the case was called out, I stood up with trembling feet. I was quite indecisive as to how to begin my address. I was lucky that as soon as I got up, the court issued a Rule and notice as to interim relief and granted ad interim relief. I could barely say just one word, "My lord". I did not understand the meaning of these legal terminologies viz. "Rule", "notice as to interim relief returnable", and "ad interim relief in terms of paragraph 9(b)". I at least understood that something very good had happened from the expressions of the other advocates present in the court. I jubilantly came out of the court and asked Ghanshyam to explain what had happened exactly. He was very kind to explain to me all those terminologies. My hands were still shivering. I tried to write the aforesaid order on the file/docket of the case but could not manage to write any sentence with my trembling hands. Anyway, it was a good beginning of my career. Thus, my actual learning of law began after this case only. I do not remember, but I charged Rs. 5000 or 10000, which was a very big amount for a person like me. After receiving the aforesaid fee, I attended court with full exuberance for a couple of months. I did not get a second case for the next ten months. But I continued diligently in my senior's office. For almost one year, I was not paid a single rupee by my senior, obviously for the reason that I was not useful to him. I could manage my survival in the profession with the fee from my first case. After one year, my senior offered me Rs. 500 as a stipend/salary, which I, with all humility, refused to accept as I was of no use to him. But he was kind to pay me Rs. 500 every month after one year.

Mr Jayant Patel left the office after two years of my joining the office. So, I thought that now I would get more and more opportunities to appear in small cases of my senior or to assist him. The things expected did not happen. I sporadically got opportunities to assist my senior. In those days my essential work was of mentioning cases and keep watch over the cases listed on the board and to call senior when our turn came. So, I was supposed to be in the court from 11 A.M to 4.45 P.M, the usual court hours. Thereafter, in the office I was expected to do small drafting and research work. Most of the time I would sit with Ghanshyam and learn from him. Now in retrospect I realise that my research was not much helpful to my senior as he had more than thirty-five years of experience in law practice, and I hardly knew anything. By the time I started getting some work from my senior, one more advocate joined my senior's office. The new advocate had some experience of drafting and of law as he had worked with one solicitor for two three years. However, for litigation practice he was completely new. He started understanding basic procedures for filing petitions, civil applications etc from me as I was his first friend in the office and that I had two and half years of experience by the time he joined. It was quite usual for him to make a friend who is junior most in the office, so I became his close friend. He called me to his home couple of times for lunch. He started gaining procedural knowledge from other colleagues also after about three four months of joining. He was competent and could successfully create an impression before our senior that he knew everything. During this period there was a marriage in the family of our senior. By his communication skill and pleasing language, he took over the responsibility of the entire marriage function. Gradually after winning the trust of our senior, he took over the responsibility of the office upon him. His general knowledge and knowledge of law was better than mine. He had a pleasing personality. He had all qualities a senior expect from a junior and he was smart too. Unfortunately, I was dumb and could not win the confidence of my senior. I was very shy and had no courage to speak to my senior. If anything is to be said to the senior I would with great hesitation put a written note on the table of my senior. In those days I was badly in need of money for survival. Under sheer circumstantial pressure I committed a mistake of putting a written note on the table of my senior that if he could pay some more salary considering the fact that the workload had increased after Mr Jayant Patel had left the office. My senior obviously did not like my timidness and the act of putting a written note on his table. If I were in the place of my senior, I would also not appreciate such a stupid thing. In those days we all colleagues would sit on the first floor of the bungalow of our senior as his office was housed on the ground floor of his bungalow. There were certain infrastructural issues on the first floor. The fan had no regulator so it would function at the top speed, the light was not enough, our senior had earlier told us that for snacks on the first floor he would make some arrangements but possibly he forgot it and some other miscellaneous issues of like nature were to be sorted out. So, we colleagues discussed those points. I do not remember exactly whether the newly joined advocate was writing down the requirements or he was telling me, and I was writing down the requirements discussed by us. Be that as it may, this written note recording the things required on the first floor of the office was brought to the notice of our senior by someone before we decided whether it should be really put up before our senior or not. I was depicted as a union leader before our senior in my absence by someone. It was projected that writing down the basic requirements on a piece of paper was my brainchild. This possibly flared up my senior. He believed the fact because of my past mistake of putting a written note on his table. During this time, I went on leave to prepare for my last LL.M examination. The only reason for doing LL.M was that I would get a part-time lectureship in a law college and get Rs.700 as an honorarium every month. I thought that Rs.700 was good for my survival. Upon completing my LL.M exams, I rejoined his office after a gap of six weeks. I did not know what had happened in the meantime in the office but the day I rejoined his office, the clerk of my senior came to me and said that I should not come to the office from the next day. I was shocked to hear this sudden snapping of my ties with the office of my senior. I was aghast by the incident. I was unceremoniously expelled from the office through the clerk named Rasikbhai without giving me an opportunity to explain, without allowing me to meet and talk to my senior. I do not blame my senior or anyone for this episode as I was partly responsible for my expulsion. The first reason perhaps was I instead of directly speaking to him about my financial difficulties wrote a note demanding more salary. The second reason seems to be the written note branded as the charter of demand. The second reason that perhaps weighed with my senior for removing me was the presentation of distorted version of the aforesaid episode. By whom?!, I do not know!

After I was thrown out of the office, I came to know that in the next couple of years two or three more colleagues in the office of my senior were also compelled to leave the office. I am not sure whether the decision to leave the office by two more advocates working in the same office was voluntary or they were expelled from the office. It is a matter of inference to be drawn from the sequence of events!

Chapter 5

Search for a New Senior

After having been thrown out from the office of my previous Senior, I started exploring options to join some other law office. In those days, I was impressed by the advocacy of Mr. Kirit Raval, who later became the Solicitor General of India. I approached him and requested to allow me to join his office. Perhaps, he did not see the spark in me. He asked me to enquire about his decision in the week thereafter. I tried to approach him, but he did not show interest, and finally, he regretted that there was no vacancy in his office. In the meantime, I came to know that there were vacancies in two other offices. Somehow, I first approached Mr. Yatin Oza (now a Senior Advocate). He was very friendly and welcomed me with great warmth. That was the most important thing for me as in the previous two offices, my importance was little more than a peon but less than a clerk. This was possibly for the reason that I was thrust upon those two seniors by circumstances. I was treated honourably in the office of Mr. Oza. He reposed trust in my capacity and started paying me Rs.1800/ – salary per month, which was to an extent enough for me to live with dignity in a society full of successful people. He started giving me enough work of drafting and arguing cases independently. Sometimes when he was out of the office, he would ask me to sit on his chair in his chamber. Getting an opportunity to sit on the chair of my senior and discussing cases with his clients boosted my confidence. In his office, I learnt the skill of filing a petition on an urgent basis and getting it circulated on the same day. Several times it so happened that we got two stages of a litigation completed in one day. In the morning, we would seek urgent circulation of a petition anytime during 11 a.m. to 1 p.m. and get it decided finally or for interim relief. If the decision was unfavourable, getting an intra-court appeal circulated on the same day. It was indeed great training and a learning experience for all his juniors. I got opportunities to argue services matters, land matters, and municipal laws matters in his office. In his office, advocates Jagdish Yadav, Brijmohan Gupta, Raj Vakil, and Hardik Rawal were my colleagues. I got along well with all of them, and I have good memories of his office. My real grooming as an advocate started from the office of Mr. Yatin Oza as I felt my existence in his office valuable.

As said earlier, I completed my LL.M just for the sake of sustaining myself in the profession. The only attraction was that if a person had an LL.M, he would usually get a part-time lectureship. I must say that while studying for my LL.M, I actually learnt law in theory. Prior to that, I was like a driver possessing a driving licence without the knowledge of driving a vehicle. I got a job as a part-time lecturer at Sir L A Shah Law College. I started earning Rs. 700 per month as expected. I was quite diffident in presenting my lectures at the law college. Moreover, every semester the principal of the college would assign new subjects to me, whether those subjects interested me or not. Being unsatisfied with the subjects assigned to me and frustrated with the scant presence of students in my class, I thought it was not worth wasting time on lecturing. The decision to leave the lectureship was partly goaded by my own limitations of language and the command over the subjects assigned to me. During the period I worked in the office of Mr. Oza, I got married to Ragini in the year 1991. In fact, I was quite sceptical about my prospects of marriage since my earnings were meagre, and I did not possess a great physique or good personality. I was thin, weighing 50 kg in those days, but fortunately, I found a bride.

During my initial years in the profession of law, one day I got an opportunity to handle a case under the Public Premises Eviction of Unauthorised Occupants Act. It was a case of one Paan Gallawala (cabin holder) who had put up his wooden cabin between two pillars of Jivan Prakash Building of Life Insurance Corporation, Relief Road (the old city area). He got a notice of eviction from the Estate Officer appointed by LIC. I prepared a reply to the notice and submitted it to the officer. The matter was kept for examination/cross-examination of the aforesaid Paanwala. I did not know much about the art of examination or cross-examination of a witness. I just told the client that whatever the officer asks, give a vague reply or deny the knowledge. At one stage of the hearing of the case, the Estate Officer, who seemed to be learnt and experienced, asked something about me to the client, and the said fellow feigned ignorance about me following my previous instructions. I was happy watching him giving answers as per my instructions. But the Estate Officer got annoyed and angrily said, "Your client is disowning you and you are smiling? What kind of lawyer are you?" I did not follow what happened but realised that something went wrong. I got embarrassed. When the written order came after the conclusion of the hearing of the case after some days, it was stated that the notice issued by LIC was legal and valid, and my client was ordered to be evicted by removing his cabin placed between two columns of the building. I told the client that he could file an appeal before the District court, but he chose not to file it for reasons best known to him. Despite the aforesaid eviction order passed thirty-five years ago, the said Paan Cabin is still there! While the aforesaid Paanwala was my client, whenever I and my wife would go to see a movie in any theatre in the old city area, I would park my scooter in front of his cabin with great pride and tell him to look after my scooter until we were back from the movie. I would thereby save a small amount of parking charge of the theatre and eat salted peanuts from the saved parking charge. I would at the same time flaunt before my wife that we could avoid paying the parking charge as the cabin holder was my client!

I worked in the office of Mr. Oza for a little more than two years. The experience of law practice that I gained in his office stood me in good stead for my future. In those days, many lawyer friends of my age would say that until you start an independent practice, you would not get clients. It was said that four years' training as a junior was fair enough to start an independent practice. I did not understand how, upon commencing independent practice, clients would start coming! My small mind was not convinced, but I was swayed by the aforementioned myth circulating among the juniors and decided to leave Mr. Oza's office without comprehending how I would survive in the profession and life. I declared to Mr. Oza that I was proposing to start my independent practice. He tried to persuade me not to make a hasty decision, knowing well that I would starve in independent practice. However, I was stubbornly stupid not to follow his advice and left his office hoping that some miracle would happen in my life.

Chapter 6

Abrupt End of My Independent Practice

One more reason that accelerated my decision to start an independent practice was that one advocate offered me to occupy a space in his office for starting my own practice. That advocate possessed an office consisting of two chambers. It was situated in a residential tower near Vijay Cross Roads, Navarangpura, Ahmedabad. Prior to his offering me one chamber, the chamber was occupied by another advocate who had taken up a job as a Legal Officer/Manager in a reputed company/ cooperative society. He had occupied the said chamber for one or one and a half years. So, the second chamber was vacant. I seized the opportunity when I was offered to occupy the second chamber as I had already decided to go for an independent practice. Besides the above fact, I was very impressed by the advocacy of that lawyer who offered me the space and thought that being a partner with that able advocate my worth would be increased. At the outset, I made it clear to the said advocate that I would not be able to pay a monthly rent or a fixed sum to him for occupying the space in his office because I had no clients. I said that whenever I would get a brief, I would part with fifteen percent of my fee towards my obligation to pay rent. He probably thought that it was a good idea without realising the fact that I had not the wherewithal to bring cases for myself. We decided to get printed common stationery, Vakalatnama, files, letterheads etc. to save avoidable expense on separate stationeries. So, the names of both of us were printed on all stationaries. Thus, my independent practice began without thinking of the consequences thereof. Whether it could be called a law practice or a recess in law practice is difficult to say!

We two shared the same office premises for approximately one year and a little more. During the entire year, I did not get a single case. Sometimes we played cricket with a ball made of a handkerchief with our hands and sometimes did percussion on the office table during the leisure time of the said advocate. The said advocate would sing, and I would do percussion on the table. He had a few clients only, whereas I had nothing but full leisure the whole day. One day some persons from a lower strata of society came to me for a case. I was desperate for a new brief and money too. I quoted a fee of about twenty thousand for all persons. The discussion lasted for forty minutes about the facts of the case and the fee to be fixed. During the discussion, the clients gained an impression that I was good for nothing. At the end of the discussion, I said that I would not charge any fee but would take up their case free of charge. Quoting a fee of twenty thousand rupees and then agreeing to do the work free of cost created doubt in their minds about my competence. Looking at my desperation, the clients went away without handing over their case to me. I became very sad on that day.

I was getting upset every day as nobody was turning up to hand over a case to me. I started thinking of various options to utilise my idle time. Finally, I decided to write a book on law. The idea of writing a book occurred to me as my brother Nishith Desai had written a book on NRI and Income Tax Benefits in the year 1984-85. That book received huge success in the circle of direct tax practitioners. His career graph had a sudden surge after the publication of his book. He became a wealthy and successful lawyer in Bombay. So, I also thought of doing specialisation in income tax and joining him. But I did not find the subject interesting. Anyway, I just decided to write a book on law for my survival. The subject I chose for my first book has an interesting background which I will reveal in the next chapter. At this stage, I would like to just inform you that the free time of this one year of my independent practice was utilised by me in writing a book on Excise Law.

It was indeed a great accomplishment for me that I could complete writing my book on Excise Law in that one year. I was expecting a magic of a flourishing practice to happen upon publication of the book, but destiny had stored something else for me. One day, the advocate with whom I was sharing his office called me to his home and declared that we were called upon to vacate the office by his father-in-law. I did not know that the property we were occupying belonged to his father-in-law. I asked him the reason for the abrupt call to vacate the office premises, to which he said that he and his wife had decided to get a divorce! I was stunned by the shocking revelation.

We vacated the office premises of the ex-father-in-law of the said advocate very quickly before we were forcibly thrown out from the office. So, I was back to square once again. Without an office space and without a brief.

The only benefit the other advocate derived by offering me a space in his office was that all printed stationery went to him for his use for the next five years after we vacated the office. I felt contented with the fact that those files bearing my name were at least found in their place on the tables of courtrooms meant for advocates' arguments since the said advocate had developed a reasonably good practice in those next five years. My name on the file lying on the court's table would bring a smile to my face as I had not achieved anything in the first five years of law practice except getting stationery printed in joint name with the aforesaid advocate.

Chapter 7

Performing the Role of an Author,
a Proofreader, a Designer, a Publisher and
a Book Seller

During the aforementioned period of struggle, I thought that there was too much competition in general law practice and that if I wanted to survive in the profession, I must specialise in any branch of law. I observed that my childhood friend Paresh Dave had carved out a niche in the field of Excise and Customs Law and was earning very well. He had a thumping practice in that branch of law and a good reputation in court being a competent advocate. He had a big office too. I saw him appearing in many cases before the high court every day. I thought that there was less competition in that branch of law which later turned out to be a myth. So, I decided to plunge into that branch of law without having experience of handling a single case of excise or customs law. I started reading the Excise Law. While reading, I realised that it was a tax on the manufacture of any product so if I wanted to practice Excise Law, I must establish contacts with manufacturers. Having no resources to contact manufacturers directly and my unwillingness to sacrifice self-respect for getting cases by directly approaching them, I decided to write a book on Excise Law to spread my name as an Excise and Customs Law practitioner among the manufacturers and the Excise Law consultants. Since I wanted to target manufacturers and thereby indirectly influence them to give their excise cases to me, I decided to write the book in Gujarati language as there was no such book available in the local language. My mediocre mind thought that since manufacturers and consultants would not understand the law in English, my book on Excise Law in Gujarati language would be sold like a hot cake. Being a briefless lawyer in those days, I spent the whole year reading and writing a book on Excise Law. It was indeed a tough job to read Excise Law and landmark judgements of the said field in English and translate the gist of the law and the judgements into Gujarati. Having no other option but to do the hard work, I could finish the book with great hopes that the publication of the book would change my fortune. Usually, if any publishing house publishes a book, the author gets 10% royalty which was not enough for my survival as I had by that time my own family of three. Moreover, I came to know that the book sellers take away 40% of the book price as their commission which I was not willing to part with. I therefore decided to publish the book myself and sell it myself and a small stock of the published book through book sellers. In fact, I wanted to get a major part of the printed price of the book for my survival. I decided on the above-mentioned course as I believed that I would earn a reasonably good amount to sustain in the profession. I had no money for publishing the book myself, so I borrowed Rs.35,000 from my friend Ashad Shah. My friend, without asking me a single question, gave me Rs.35,000 as he had full trust not in my ability but honesty. I myself designed the cover page, did proofreading, purchased papers through Bal Govind Kuberdas & Co, found out a printing press and a binder. Finally, I got the book printed with a black cover page designed by myself. To me, the cover was quite attractive. But in retrospect, if I think about the design of the cover page, it was not as attractive as I believed it to be. So, to avoid embarrassment that the author himself was the publisher, I created a one-book publishing company named "R. S. Publishers". The word 'R' was taken from the initials of my wife Ragini, and the word 'S' was taken from the initials of my daughter Shaivaa. I requested

Hon'ble Justice S B Majmudar to write a Foreword for the book. He, with some reluctance, agreed to do it and obliged me. I also requested the President of the Gujarat Chamber of Commerce to write about my book. He also obliged me by writing a good review of my book. Similarly, one more association of manufacturers was asked to write a review and the same was also made part of my book. The whole idea of doing this was to spread my name amongst industrialists and Excise Law consultants through whom I could get cases.

When the book came into my hands after its publication, I kept staring at it for five minutes. I had the same feeling a mother usually has when she gives birth to a baby and the baby is placed in her hand. I was quite elated with the publication of the book but did not realise where to store the stock of one thousand copies of the book. I got all the books dumped in the office which I was sharing with the other advocate I spoke about. I thought of arranging a book release function to gain some popularity in the profession. I wanted to make the book release function very grand so that it would attract the attention of the media. I chose to invite the Minister of Industries to release the book. The Minister agreed to grace the occasion. The date and time of the book release function were fixed. However, at the last moment, the Minister sent a message that he would not be able to grace the function. I got upset with the sudden refusal of the Minister. I, therefore, at the last moment requested justice N.J. Pandya who was known to me to grace the function. He was very kind to agree to grace the book release function. I also requested Senior Standing Counsel Mr. Haroo Mehta to be a guest of honour. He also agreed to be part of the book release function. I held the book release function in the Gujarat Sahitya Parishad Hall. I made sure that the function was followed by ice-cream so that more advocates come to attend the function. Finally, the book release function was held with the presence of approximately seventy-five to a hundred attendees. I was happy with the presence of whatever number of invitees who were kind enough to attend my function. I must have spent a total of forty thousand rupees for the publication of the book, including the book release function. Fortunately, the function went reasonably well, and I became an author, a young author aged 29. I became known to some extent in the Gujarat High Court after the publication of the book.

As said earlier, I thought that my books would be sold like hot cakes, which did not happen. On the day of the book release, only about 25 to 30 books were sold. The real difficulty started after the book release function. The book sellers said that they purchase law books on a "sale or return" basis and would pay me only upon the actual sale of my book. The book sellers hardly purchased ten copies of my book on their own terms. I got disappointed and dejected temporarily. I then realised how difficult it would be to sell one thousand copies of my book. But I did not lose my hopes. I went to the Gujarat Chamber of Commerce and bought the Gujarat manufacturers directory containing the addresses and telephone numbers of all manufacturers. I gave an advertisement in a newspaper to appoint a salesman. I took personal interviews of many salespersons and finally selected one person. I took my wife's help in writing letters to manufacturers asking them to place an order for my book. When any order is received, my wife would go to Navarngpura Post Office in the city bus with a bundle of books and dispatch the books to the manufacturers who had ordered the book. Finally, with great difficulties, I could get rid of the substantial stock of my book and reach the breakeven point. From the money received from the sale of the books, I could sustain myself in the profession of law for one and a half years as my needs were very little. I could also recover the investment made by me in this project by borrowing Rs.35,000 from my dear friend Ashad and could return Rs.35,000 to him, who never ever reminded me to return the money. I cannot forget this act of kindness of Ashad and will remain indebted to him forever.

During my initial career, at one stage when I was doing nothing, I joined justice A R Dave's (Retd. Supreme Court Judge), who was the solicitor for the State of Gujarat. I joined his office to gain experience in handling cases for the government. He also made it clear that since his bills were not being cleared by the government on a regular basis, he would not promise any stipend to me. So, the deal was open-ended; if he received his bills, he might pay a stipend of Rs. 700 or 1000. He was a thorough gentleman and very humble. I worked under him for about six months and gained experience in the field of labour law cases. I enjoyed working under him, though for a very brief span.

After the publication of my aforementioned book, I got an opportunity to join the firm named Trivedi & Gupta. It was a firm of Mr. Kamal Trivedi (now Advocate General) and Mr. Rakesh Gupta, advocate. It was a leading firm dealing with the cases pertaining to Excise and Customs laws. Although I was not assured that I would deal with excise or customs cases in his firm, I joined his office as I had no other options for survival. I was given to understand that I would be paid Rs. 2500 monthly. I worked in that firm for one or two months only for the reasons mentioned hereunder.

One fine day, the opportunity knocked on my door. While I was working with the firm Trivedi and Gupta, my ex-colleague advocate Hardik Rawal one day said that he had a very good acquaintance with Mr. S.I. Nanavati and he could recommend my name if I wanted to join his office. He said that in Mr. S.I. Nanvati's office, I would get an attractive salary but the condition would be that I could not do my private practice. I was in dire need of money to maintain my family, and I had no private practice, so I expressed my willingness to join the office of Mr. S. I. Nanavati, a well-known lawyer. I was quick in my decision since I realised in five years of law practice that I had no potential to develop my own private practice. I was full of exuberance to join the office of Mr. S.I. Nanavati as I was to look after excise and customs cases in his office, and that my financial worries were likely to be over by joining his office. In my view, joining Mr. S.I. Nanavati's office was a turning point for my career and life.

Chapter 8

"Saala Mein to Saab Ban Gaya", My Exposure to the Elite Class Culture of My New Senior

I was to join the office of Mr. S I Nanavati from the first of March 1994 but before I joined, I got a call from his office on the festival day of Holi that I was required to attend a meeting in Delhi with advocate Shridharan regarding an Excise Law case. I could not believe those words as I was to travel on an aeroplane for the first time in my life. I did not have a good travel bag at home for air travel. Fortunately, I found a bag from VIP Company brought by my wife at the time of our marriage. It was not in very good condition, full of dust and scratches. So, I asked my wife to wipe it with a wet cloth to make it shine. My wife did that job perfectly, and I was ready for my first flight to New Delhi. I reached the airport in an autorickshaw. I managed to complete the check-in formalities at the counter, which were obviously new to me. I sat in the aeroplane and observed how people were fastening their seatbelts. I did not face difficulty in fastening the seatbelt. I was excited to watch the sky and the view of the earth from the aeroplane. I constantly gazed outside the window of the aeroplane and felt on top of the hill. I was to accompany other advocates for the conference with the Delhi Lawyer as I was completely a novice in the field of Excise and Customs Law. After reaching Delhi, we were taken to The Claridges Hotel situated on Aurangzeb Road (Now the name of the road has been changed). My little eyes were dazzled by the riches I saw when we checked into the above-named five-star hotel. I carried a towel and dental kit with me in the bag as I did not know that the hotel would provide such things. It was a dream-like experience for me. On the next day, we set out for a meeting with the Delhi Advocate Mr. Shridharan. During the meeting, I spoke one or two sentences and tried to justify my presence and the expense to the client for taking me to Delhi. I do not remember whether my inputs were useful or not, but I had great satisfaction in being considered worth sending to Delhi by my Senior Mr. S I Nanavati. It was a memorable travel to and staying in Delhi.

After my first visit to New Delhi, I was exposed to a completely new world of rich people. Thereafter, in some time, I became a frequent flyer and started earning bonus points that entitled me to free tickets. In those days, the excise and customs Tribunals were in Delhi and for the western region in Bombay. Certain types of cases would go to the Delhi tribunal, and certain types of cases would go to the regional bench in Bombay. In Bombay, usually, I would stay at the Oberoi Hotel at Nariman Point and in Delhi at Taj Mansingh, obviously not at my cost. Initially, when I started staying in five-star hotels, the hotel staff would come to know from my attire and the luggage I carried that I was not five-star material. At the time of checking in, the receptionist would embarrass me by asking me to give my credit card to block a certain amount to ensure that I had sufficient means to pay the hotel bill. My answer was that I had no credit or debit card. For possessing a credit card, one should have good financial credentials and for a debit card one should have a bank balance; I had neither of these two. So, they would ask me to deposit cash security to which I would readily comply with from the money given to me from my senior's office. I must say that those experiences were really embarrassing for me. Therefore, to avoid such discomfiture, I would write a communication on the previous day of my journey to the hotel manager on the letterhead of my senior and get the signature of my senior on it. Before reaching

Delhi or Bombay, I would ask our office clerk to fax it to the hotel. Mr. S. I. Nanavati was a privileged guest for all five-star hotels in Delhi and Bombay. Once a letter under his signature was received before my checking in any hotel, nobody would dare to ask me to deposit any amount for my stay in the hotel. This mechanism worked well as the communication contained a message to the hotel manager that the person who was going to stay in the hotel was an advocate from his office. I must have stayed in all reputed five-star hotels like Oberoi Delhi, Oberoi Bombay, Taj Mansingh Delhi, Taj Gateway of India Bombay, Holiday Inn, Hyatt, Trident, Lalit, Leela, Taj Palace, and Maurya Sheraton, and so on and so forth during my practice as a junior to Mr. S. I. Nanavati. These luxurious stays and travels I experienced in the office of Mr. S.I. Nanavati gave me the feelings of the Bollywood song *"Saala mein to saab ban gaya, re saab ban ke kesa tun gaya"*. Though, from inside, I knew that standalone nobody would have spent a penny on me. I was quite conscious of the fact that I could wallow in these luxuries only because I was a junior to Mr. S. I. Nanavati.

Sometimes I travelled in business class in the company of my Senior or sometimes without him. The paradox was that I would reach the airport on my scooter or in an autorickshaw but would travel in an aeroplane many a time in business class and stay in a five-star hotel. The people sitting in the business class would think that I must be a rich person or a person of some eminence and pass a typical smile which an unknown rich person passes on to another unknown rich person. I would sometimes talk like a rich business tycoon with fellow passengers on board discussing the issues of the Indian economy, global warming, and poor work culture prevalent in our society and other such larger issues. Only I knew my financial condition and the fact that I used to reach the airport on my scooter or in an autorickshaw. Being an experienced air traveller and now fully well-versed with five-star culture, I would act like rich people while staying in hotels too.

With the money given by my Senior, I would generously give tips to bellboys or room service waiters or butlers imitating my senior.

I would like to share one hilarious incident that happened to me. One day there was a friendly cricket match between film stars and cricketers sponsored by Sahara Group Company in Delhi. They all were to stay, or actually staying, in Hotel Taj Mansingh in Delhi. Coincidentally, I was to reach Taj Mansingh on that very day. There was a huge crowd in the porch area of the hotel to have a glimpse of their favourite film star or cricketer. It so happened that on that day the hotel sent a brand-new black Mercedes to pick me up from the airport. When the Mercedes carrying me entered the porch of the hotel, the crowd cheered up, expecting that a cricketer or a film star would get down from the car. But when they saw me, a frail young unknown person getting down from the car, they booed me as I belied their expectations and disappointed them with my entry. It was my hooting entry in the hotel. I still laugh at this incident, remembering the exact scene.

I also vividly remember another such hilarious incident. Another day, to save money to reach Hotel Taj Mansingh from the Supreme Court by taxi, I asked our clerk, Subhash, to drop me on his scooter to Hotel Taj. It was in the month of April, so there was no possibility of rain. But suddenly, the atmosphere became cloudy and before we could think, it started raining heavily. I got completely drenched in the rain. I got down at the exit gate of the Hotel to avoid the embarrassment of being noticed by the people staying in the hotel and the hotel staff that I had reached the hotel on a scooter. From the exit gate, I reached the porch area of the hotel with wet clothes. I entered Hotel Taj fully soaked with rainwater. I made the whole foyer, the floor, and the elevator wet and soiled. I felt very awkward for the whole episode. On that day, I did not get down to the ground floor for dinner in the restaurant and kept myself confined to the room by ordering the meal there.

I was a diffident person suffering from an inferiority complex. The main reasons were: I was very thin, underweight, did not have a sound financial condition, had studied in Gujarati medium, was not a brilliant student, did not possess great expression power, and lacked fluency in English. However, gradually I became confident with the exposure to the five-star culture in the office of Mr. S.I. Nanavati. It was the policy of Mr. Nanavati that his juniors should also have a status in society, and therefore he would give a car to his juniors if a junior stays in his office for a sufficiently long time. I really admire his policy. After three years in the office of Mr. Nanavati, I was given a second-hand car, Maruti 800. It was a second-hand car because another employee was given a new car due to his long association with Mr. Nanavati, and the earlier car given to him was lying idle. I was excited to have a car which I had never dreamt of. Upon my exposure to the new world and getting a car from Mr. Nanavati, I started gaining confidence in life and the profession. People started becoming nice to me. I must admit that my grooming actually started in the office of Mr. S.I. Nanavati, and I am indeed grateful to him.

While I was working under Mr. S. I Nanavati, I kept on revising the book on Excise Law from 1994-1997. After the self-publication of the book, one publisher from Bombay agreed to publish my book every year. I was very happy because I did not have to worry about the sale of the book. Gradually, word spread in the legal circle that I was an author and possessed an in-depth knowledge of Excise and Customs Law. I received an invitation from the Customs House Agents' association to deliver a lecture on the issues they were facing while importing goods. Without understanding the intricacies of the topic, I seized the opportunity to deliver my first lecture. I had some experience of delivering lectures in law college and hence thought that I would be able to manage. However, the topic was quite difficult as it required knowledge of the procedural aspects of customs law. Anyhow, I prepared the lecture and started with trembling feet to the venue. Fortunately, a thunderstorm came, and it rained heavily on that day in Ahmedabad. I was not worried by the heavy rain. On the contrary, I was happy inside. I thought it was better if only a few people could reach the venue of my lecture. I thought that in such an eventuality, my ignorance would be exposed to a smaller number of people. The lecture was attended by hardly twenty to thirty persons. I do not remember how I started my lecture and how I completed it. But I am sure that it was quite unimpressive. If more people had attended the lecture, the organisers would have regretted calling me to deliver the lecture as an expert. Anyway, the rain saved me from being exposed of my ignorance of law and language.

Similarly, after the union budget for the year 1996 was passed, I got an invitation from the Surat Textile Manufacturers and Processors' Association to deliver a lecture on the changes brought in the Excise Law by the Finance Act, 1996. I prepared my speech to the best of my ability. While I was travelling on the train to reach Surat for the aforementioned lecture, I thought that my lecture should be very interesting. I thought that I should add humour to my lecture to make it interesting. I had in the past once heard the budget speech delivered by the eminent lawyer and jurist Nani Palkhivala. A queer thought came to my mind that like Nani Palkhivala, I should also give the facts and figures from the union budget and should try to imitate him. Quite oblivious to my limited knowledge and other limitations, I wanted the audience to be spellbound by my lecture. So, my lecture was full of facts, figures, and details. But at the last moment, a strange idea of adding humour crept into my mind which ultimately spoiled the lecture. More than three hundred persons had gathered to hear something very serious from the speakers on the budget proposals and the Finance Act. They were not ready for the humour, and I started the lecture with something humorous. I think not a single person laughed in the audience or appreciated the humour. Having realised this mistake, I immediately switched over to the serious part of the lecture, but by that time, it was too late. My budget lecture did not evoke a good response from the audience. So, my first two public lectures were utter failures but quite useful from the point of gaining experience of public speaking.

Somehow, my mind was wandering for doing something new and which can generate additional stable income. My Senior Mr. S. I. Nanavati is the main trustee of the Gujarat Law Society which runs more than thirty educational institutions. I, therefore, suggested to him to start a certificate course in Excise Law under the banner of the Gujarat Law Society. He found my idea interesting and accepted it. I became the Director of the GLS Institute of Excise Law. I thought he would offer me a handsome remuneration for the post of director but, the amount that was offered was meagre. The course evoked a very good response. In the first batch, sixty students got enrolled and I taught them Excise Law. Certificates were issued to them upon completing the course. The aforementioned course lasted for one term as I lost interest in it because of the meagre remuneration offered to me.

I would like to share an interesting arbitration case I handled in the office of Mr. S. I. Nanavati. It was a case concerning a contractual dispute between ONGC and our client regarding the Sagar Lakshmi Oil Project. The arbitration was taking place in Bombay. It is noteworthy that one of the arbitrators was from Ahmedabad, the claimant's advocate (us) was from Ahmedabad, and the opponent's advocate, Ms. V. P. Shah, was also from Ahmedabad, but the seat/venue of the arbitration was in Bombay. Before I was assigned to handle this case, it had been managed by three other advocates from his office, all of whom, for one reason or another, left the office within three years. Nevertheless, the arbitration was ongoing. I commenced handling the arbitration case with my senior, Mr. S. I. Nanavati. The subject matter was new to me.

Some lawyers unfamiliar with arbitration law would inquire how arbitration works, and I would explain that we need to go to the venue, sit through the arbitration, have a cup of tea/coffee with snacks initially, then lunch in two hours, and the arbitration proceeds automatically. This was my understanding of arbitration law!

When I joined that arbitration case, the arbitration was being conducted in the Belveder Club in Hotel Oberoi. It was quite a costly affair for our client. He was required to bear business class tickets for Mr. Nanavati and me and hotel stay for both of us in separate rooms. Economy class fare for our stenographer who would stay with me in my room. In the morning around 10.30, the arbitration would start. The judicial arbitrator was once the Chief Justice of Gujarat High Court. He was fond of food and well-travelled. As soon as we assembled for the arbitration, tea, coffee, juice, cookies, and sandwiches would be served. During this time, the arbitrator would share his experiences of his stay in different cities, different hotels, and the speciality of the city or the hotel and the food served there. Such talk would consume approximately forty-five minutes to one hour every time. Actual arbitration would start at 11.30. The proceedings would be conducted up to 1 P.M, and then we would have a lunch break. The lunch break would last for one and a half hours. We would reassemble at 2.30 P.M. The arbitration would start for one hour, and then the discussion on the next date of the arbitration. The discussion on the availability of both the arbitrators, the claimant's lawyer, and opponent's lawyer would again consume forty-five minutes to one hour, and we would disperse by 4 P.M. so as to catch our evening flight, keeping in mind the distance from the Hotel Oberoi to the airport. I must have attended this arbitration for one year. The arbitration in Belveder Club in Hotel Oberoi turned out to be very expensive for the clients, so the clients requested to change the venue of arbitration to Hotel Kohinoor in the Prabhadevi area of Bombay. So, we ended up doing arbitration in Hotel Kohinoor. However, we still continued to fly in business class and stay in Oberoi or Taj. So, the client did not save any substantial amount. This arbitration continued even after I left the office of Mr. Nanavati. I am not sure about the truth of the fact, but I was informed by someone that the arbitration was proved to be so costly that our client, who owned a business, became broke and had to take employment somewhere else. I have no information on whether the final award was ever passed by the arbitrators!

After having four years' experience in Mr S.I. Nanavati's office, the thoughts of establishing my own name in the profession started hovering in my mind. I declared that I would leave the office within two months. The funny part was that I made the aforesaid declaration in the office before making arrangements for an independent practice. A thought struck to join Vijay Patel advocate's office, who was an elected MP and had nobody to look after his office. I had no close acquaintance with him but just knew that he had good contacts and a law practice. I went to meet him but returned without meeting him, thinking how I could propose a partnership without knowing him. Finally, I mustered the courage, thinking that at worst he would refuse and say 'no'. I went back to meet him and proposed a partnership with him. Fortunately, he was in need of somebody who was a reliable advocate and who could look after his office, as he was busy in active politics and his firm was running at a loss.

I went to my Senior Mr. S. I. Nanavati and gave him back the key of the car given by him to me. I expressed my gratitude to him for giving me opportunities to bloom. He expressed that he would not mind paying a higher salary and asked me to stay for some more years in his office. But I respectfully informed him that I was joining Advocate Mr. Vijay Patel as his partner in his law firm. Mr. Nanavati conveyed best wishes to me.

Chapter 9

Back to Scooter From Car

It was difficult for me to get back to the scooter from the car. I joined the office of Mr. Vijay Patel as his partner. Since he had the goodwill of his father and a reasonable practice, we decided to share the profit and loss in the ratio of 60:40. I was not required to make any investment in the office. It was his office, his goodwill, and his contacts. I was to take care of the office and run it efficiently. The loss-making firm started making a profit from the first month itself. We earned approximately Rs. 28,000 in the first month, which was shared by us in the above-stated proportion. The amount that came to my share was almost equal to what I was getting in Mr. S.I. Nanavati's office.

In no time, we started earning well. Mr. Vijay Patel was a very nice person. He had full trust in my ability and honesty. He would remain actively involved in politics, which would bring many clients to our firm. I would work very hard on each case that came to us, so clients were very happy. It was like a story of a blind man and a person having no legs. They were to reach a destination on foot at the same place. But both had their own handicaps. Both of them, therefore, decided that the person having no legs would sit on the shoulder of the blind man and the blind man would walk as directed by the person sitting on his shoulder having a vision. I was unable to walk in law practice but had the capacity and ability to see. On the other hand, Vijay Patel had many clients because of his active politics and on account of the goodwill of his father late Mr. H.L Patel, who was also a successful lawyer and politician. Mr. Vijay Patel was unable to devote his time to law practice and develop it, though he was fully competent. So, metaphorically it can be said that he had no vision. I climbed on his shoulder, and he would walk as per my vision. The combination worked very well. The partnership started flourishing. I started getting recognition in court because of frequent appearances. It took ten years of law practice to make my presence felt among the judges and the lawyers of Gujarat High Court. Finally, I could establish my identity as a good lawyer due to my partnership with Mr. Vijay Patel. I would remain indebted forever to Mr. Vijay Patel for accepting me as his partner, giving me full autonomy to run his office and appear in all cases that came to the firm.

In the year 1998-99, Mr. Kirit Rawal, an eminent advocate of Gujarat High Court, became the Additional Solicitor General and later Solicitor General in the Supreme Court of India. Mr. Vijay Patel had very close relations with him. Mr. Kirit Rawal asked Mr. Vijay Patel to suggest some names for the appointment as Standing Counsels for the Central government for representing the central government in the High Court of Gujarat. Mr. Vijay Patel suggested some names, including my name. I became an Additional Standing Counsel not on merit but due to my association with Vijay Patel, a Member of Parliament. I must mention one important incident of my career. This incident highlights the fact that unless you are politically strong or have good relations with the persons or bureaucrats in power, you do not get any government post. At one stage of my career without anybody's support or acquaintance (maybe between years 1993 to 1997), I tried very hard to become an Assistant Government Pleader, but nobody thought me worth for that office. I approached the Government Pleader of that time through someone for getting an appointment to the post of an Assistant Government Pleader, but I did not get it. I even indirectly approached the Chief Minister, Mr. Dilip Parikh, through someone who was close to the CM for getting an appointment to the post of Assistant Government Pleader, but I was not appointed as an Assistant Government Pleader. The reason was obvious that I did not belong to the groups of influential people. As against that, the office of Additional Central Government Standing Counsel (ACGSC) came to me without any effort merely because I was the partner of Vijay Patel, a Member of Parliament!

I worked as ACGSC from 1998 up to 2004. In 2004, the BJP lost in the centre, and I immediately resigned from the post of an Additional Central Government Counsel to facilitate the new government to appoint their own team of Central government Counsels. But these six years of conducting cases as an Additional Central Government Counsel proved very useful and enriching. I got opportunities to conduct excise, customs, NDPS, and other important cases for the central government. Mr. Vijay Patel and I remained partners in the firm H L Patel Advocates for seventeen years. During these seventeen years, many interesting things happened which I have narrated as separate topics.

Chapter 10

Starting Practice From Scratch Again

In the year 2012-2013, the son of Mr. Vijay Patel became an advocate. After one year of his joining the firm, the question arose as to what should be his share as a partner. I was not willing to reduce my share in the firm after successfully running the firm for seventeen years, and if Mr. Vijay Patel reduced his share, it would be unfair to him. So, we decided that his son should be made a partner in the firm, and I should retire from the firm. We decided that I would retire from the firm with effect from 1st November 2013. I would not take a single case file from the firm H L Patel Advocates as most of the cases came to us because of his contacts and public relations. We decided that after leaving the firm, I would not contact any of his clients and solicit work from his contacts. I would also not contact the briefing advocates who I knew due to Mr. Vijay Patel. I said that since I was retiring from the firm suddenly, that too without taking a single brief from the firm, Mr. Vijay Patel should pay me seventy-five thousand rupees per month for the next one year, and in reciprocation, I would conduct the hearing of some cases that may be assigned to me by him. For three months, he paid me the agreed amount without giving me any case to argue as it was perhaps not found feasible. Thus, the aforesaid arrangement lasted for three months. By that time the clients started searching for me and coming to me without my solicitation. I started earning well. I have no grievance for the non-payment of the agreed amount from Mr. Vijay Patel because I believe that my substantial existence in the profession and the position I have today in society is due to my long association with Mr. Vijay Patel. I am indeed grateful to Mr. Vijay Patel for all I received in my professional career.

I could survive on my own because of the grace of the universe (as I am an atheist), the blessing of my late parents from the sky (as I don't believe in heaven), and the hard work I had done in the law practice for the last twenty-four years.

Thus, I actually started my practice as an independent advocate from 1st November 2013. I started practising from the court-allotted chamber No. 322 for four months. It was my dream to have my own independent office since the day I entered the profession. I started searching for an office nearby the high court and finally found one in the building known as Shapath Hexa. When I started practising independently, two advocates, viz. Advocate Jay Sunilbhai Shah and advocate Manan Bhatt, joined my office. One client came with his nephew named Gaurav Vyas and asked me if his nephew could be accommodated in my office for any work. The client said that his nephew knew shorthand and he would do typing work and also work as a stenographer. The boy started doing paralegal work in my office. After some time, he was inspired to pursue LL.B and he became a lawyer. He worked with me for nearly ten years, and now he has also started his own practice, bought a car, and booked his own flat. I am happy that he could stand on his own legs. Jay Shah also started his own practice after seven years of working with me and has marched on a successful career. Jay will certainly become a successful lawyer as his understanding is very good. Advocate Manan Bhatt is an avid reader and a successful advocate doing independent practice from my office. I have many hopes for him and wish that he becomes a high court judge someday. Now Shyam Shah is also part of my office. He is also a very competent advocate, and my best wishes to him too.

Chapter 11

Some Unpleasant Experiences From Judges and Police Officers Moulded My Career

While I was a partner with Mr Vijay Patel and was working as an Additional Central Government Counsel, one particular judge constantly harassed me for no reason. As soon as I would get up for conducting a case, he would insult me and get angry with me. In one case, because of a personal grudge against me, he issued a contempt notice to a Joint Director General of Foreign Trade who was posted in Calcutta. The officer got worried as it would mar his service career. I told him not to worry as I was sure that he had not committed contempt of court. The Joint Director of Foreign Trade, who was asked to remain personally present, was nervous and trembling in the court which had issued the contempt notice. When the case was listed before the same bench and was taken up for hearing, I mustered the courage and took an objection before the aforesaid judge that his bench was entitled to issue a notice for contempt but he would be required to send it to the bench taking up the contempt matters as per the roster. The judge got annoyed but realised that he was not empowered to proceed further and hence directed it to be listed before the bench taking up contempt matters. The officer who was present did not follow what happened. I explained to him and asked him not to worry. When the case was listed before the bench taking up contempt matters, I was not even called upon to utter a single word and the notice for contempt of court was discharged. There were many such instances of receiving improper treatment from some judges by me and many lawyers. Such instances prompted me to think about the course of action available to a lawyer against such improper behaviour. I did not know where to make a complaint so thought of penning down my bruised feeling in the form of an article. I wrote my first article titled as "How is a judge expected to conduct himself in the temple of justice" which was published in the law journal All India Reporter. The article contained many bold and controversial statements borrowed from some judgements or from books. The following paragraph borrowed from the book "Professional Deformities" by George Mike was liked by many lawyers:

"It was not that judges were, or are, sadists. Very few of them are. But sooner or later most of them develop a God complex. When everyone keeps kowtowing to you; when people laugh at your silliest jokes and listen to your most trivial utterances as though they were the Sermon on the Mount; when the outcome of quarrels and arguments, and often the fates of men, women and their children rest in your hands; when you cannot be sacked from your job however incompetent or senile you become… When, in other words, you are treated like God, then it is difficult not to believe in your own divinity. You are addressed as "my lord", almost like Him, so naturally you are inclined to believe he is your colleague. I should point out, however, that this rule, like all rules, lacks universal validity. I have known cunning geese. I have met naïve foxes. And I have known modest and almost human judges."

One of the judges of the high court appreciated my article in the presence of the judge who used to insult me. When he was asked to comment on the article by his brother judge, he said that writing articles was a job of idle and briefless lawyers and he would never read such trash material. I think the message reached him loud and clear, but he was haughty and therefore unwilling to appreciate it and improve himself. I received a letter from a very Senior Advocate, Mr. Pavecha, from Indore showering praises on me for being a bold and fearless advocate. He expressed willingness to meet me and said that when he happened to be in Ahmedabad, he would definitely meet me. He came to my office, and the said relation of mutual respect is still lasting. I am of the firm view that to bring out the full potential of a lawyer, the existence of bad judges is of equal importance as good judges. Bad or tough judges will require you to prepare your case to the best of your ability thoroughly. They prepare you for the most difficult questions to answer during the hearing of a case. Such judges go to an absurdity in asking you questions and try to humiliate. But such judges make you strong if you take such things in the right way. Whereas good judges keep your morale very high by giving you patient hearing, extending courtesy, and speaking encouraging words. I have noticed that my preparation was best when I was to face such haughty and bad-tempered judges. But I would perform best before decent and good judges where I was made comfortable by such judges.

The aforesaid unexpected favourable response from the legal fraternity inspired me to write a book on the law of contempt of court as I thought that it was the contempt power of judges which needed to be understood first if I wanted to practice law with dignity and respect. I wanted to know to what extent I could criticise judges for their misbehaviour within and without the court. I started collecting case laws on the topic of contempt of court. I studied many books on contempt of court written by Indian authors and other foreign authors. This time I did not commit the same mistake of becoming a publisher and a book seller myself. I was earning reasonably in those days so I was happy about the prospects of receiving ten percent royalty for the books sold. I requested the late Justice Mr. R. K. Abichandani who was an academician and learnt judge to write a "Foreword" for the book. He could understand with his experienced eyes that the book had many flaws but he did not want to disappoint me. He drew my attention to some of the mistakes in the book, asked me to read some foreign decisions. He thereafter wrote the Foreword for the book. The book was published in the year 2003 by SnowWhite Publishers, Bombay. In my view, the book was very average. It was like a compilation of the case law arranged by me in proper sequence by giving appropriate headings. It contained sporadic comments as an author on certain topics. But this book established my identity as an author, academician, and scholar. Only, I knew that there was nothing scholarly in the book. People usually do not read books closely and analytically. They judge the book by the cover page, the number of pages, judgements of the Supreme Court, High Courts referred to therein and who wrote the Foreword for the book. Fortunately, the publisher made the cover page very attractive and the book contained all the material an advocate usually wants. So, I got the stamp of an author from the members of the Bar. I started gaining acceptance in the legal circle and among judges as an academician and scholar. My acceptance by the legal fraternity as an author encouraged me to revise this book and try to correct mistakes made by me in the first edition of the book. In the revised editions of the years 2010 and 2021, I corrected all mistakes, analysed each topic, rearranged them in proper sequence, added my personal views wherever possible. Today I can confidently say that the book has now indeed become a scholarly product having great worth.

Two bad experiences of the police engendered the seeds of writing a book on the rights of arrested persons, powers of the investigating officer, and bail. Somewhere before twenty-five years, one day I received a call from my wife's cousin that he had met with an accident and in the accident on a highway, a small boy had died. I asked him the details of the incident. He said that on the highway, he was driving his car at a speed of 70 or 80 km per hour, but one boy who was carrying the herd of sheep and goats with his father on the highway suddenly ran towards the opposite side of the road. My wife's cousin's car hit the boy.

My wife's cousin stopped his car, got down from the car, and took the boy to the nearest hospital, but the boy died. He approached the police station and informed the police about the accident. The case would attract Section 279 or at best 304A of the IPC. Both offences were bailable, but the police asked for Rs. 1500 from my wife's cousin and said that he would allow my wife's cousin to go home, but he would have to report to the police station the next day. He would be produced before the Magistrate on the next day, and the Magistrate would grant bail even though the offence was bailable. My wife's cousin was made to pay Rs. 1500 for his early production before the Magistrate. On the next day when a copy of the FIR was given to us, to our shock, totally false facts were found in the FIR. The FIR contained a statement that the driver ran away after the accident. This incident of the police harassing a citizen to undergo the process of obtaining bail from the Magistrate in a bailable offence case shocked my conscience. I felt helpless. I was hurt. I turned a blind eye to my wife's cousin giving the bribe of fifteen hundred to the police officer in the campus of the police station itself. But the hurt feelings did not go away from my heart and mind for a considerably long time.

Just within one or two years of the said incident, the police intervened in the matter pertaining to the dispute about the fee to be charged by a doctor from another doctor for the surgery. The doctor who underwent the surgery was my client. The police said that they would arrest my client if the fee was not paid. I asked for the details of the FIR, if any. The police officer said that there was no FIR, but he had received a complaint from the doctor who had performed surgery on my client. When I resisted the illegal attempt of the police officer to settle the dispute about the exact amount of the fee to be paid by my client to the doctor, he said he would book me for the offence under Section 186 of IPC, which is non-cognisable and bailable but in the State of Gujarat cognisable and non-bailable. This led me to write an article on the topic of whether a preliminary inquiry is permissible under the provisions of the Criminal Procedure Code, 1973. I did good research and found that the police had no authority to conduct an investigation in the garb of a preliminary inquiry without registering a formal FIR. My article answers many important questions that are not found in the judgement which was given by the Supreme Court almost ten years later in *Lalita Kumari vs State of UP AIR 2014 SC 187*.

The aforesaid two incidents of the abuse of police power finally made me write a book titled "rights of arrested persons, Investigation and Bail" in the year 2006. This book again could not be considered a great book. It was an average book providing most useful details on the topics dealt with therein. This book did not pick up in the market because of its long title. I realised that nobody would ask for or inquire about a book on the rights of arrested persons or simply on the topic of investigation. On the topic of bail, there may be inquiries from many, but the topic of Bail was mentioned last in the title of my book. So, the book mostly remained on the shelves of the library and in the godown of the publisher. I corrected this mistake in the year 2013 and wrote a book exclusively on the topic of Bail. This book picked up well, and my personal views on many topics expressed in the book later received the imprimatur of the Supreme Court of India.

The book on the subject "Writs and other Constitutional Remedies" was also the product of my certain unpleasant experiences as a high court lawyer. During twenty years of my practice at that time, I noticed that the jurisdiction of Article 226 and 227 of the Constitution is exercised in a most arbitrary manner. Whether a petition filed by a litigant would be entertained or not by the court still depends on the constitution, tamper and prejudice of a judge described as discretion. Though there are well-recognised principles of law with regard to the exercise of the jurisdiction under articles 226 and 227, the said principles are not followed by judges. I also noticed that applying the technicalities associated with the traditional Writs, some courts would dismiss a petition without examining the substance of the grievance on merit. Moreover, there was a permanent legal question whether the judge exercised jurisdiction under Article 226 or Article 227 of the Constitution of India and whether an intra-court appeal would be maintainable or not. On all the above issues, there are contradictory judgements of high courts and the Supreme Court of India. I, therefore, thought of understanding the nature of the high court's jurisdiction for my clarity and for the clarity of all concerned. I, therefore, started collecting the case law on the topic and made in-depth research. I completed the work of writing the above book in three years. I sent the manuscript to Taxman, a reputed publisher, and made an offer to publish my book. After some time, Taxman rejected my offer and refused to publish my aforesaid book. I got disappointed by the rejection and did introspection. I went through the book again and substantially modified it with my personal views on important topics. The book was finally accepted by LexisNexis Butterworths for its publication. In this book, I evolved a new theory for resolving many issues surrounding the requirement of entertaining a petition as a matter of right or as a discretion. The theory is described as the "Theory of direct/substantial violation of a fundamental right or indirect/incidental violation". Many new concepts were introduced in the book. I received many accolades for this book. Fortunately, in *Kaushal Kishor's vs. State of UP 2023 (4) SCC 1* the analysis of fundamental rights in a tabular form has been done substantially in the same manner as done in my book. But the aforesaid theory evolved by me in the book has not yet been applied by any court in practice!

I have written many articles on different topics of law where I found that the Supreme Court's decision did not appeal to my common sense or unjust. Some of them have found imprimatur of the Supreme Court in the later years. Still, some are awaiting the approval of the Supreme Court.

Chapter 12

Buying First Home with Borrowed Money From Friends and Relatives

During the year 1996, my wife and I decided to separate from my parents' home. The decision was not for any good reason. Since my childhood, my father insisted on following the rules of discipline he made for all family members. He would frequently say that if anyone did not want to follow those rules, he or she would be free to leave the home. While I was earning Rs. 8000 per month in the office of Mr. Nanavati, one day for a trivial reason, my father said that my wife and I should abide by the discipline of the home, and if we could not, we were free to leave home. Out of anger, my wife Ragini and I decided to leave my parents' home. We began searching for a rented house. Finally, we found one house in Nanarnpura area at the rent of Rs. 3200 per month. It was the first floor of a bungalow with a small terrace. On the ground floor, the old landlady was staying. We started living there happily. The salary was sufficient to sustain our living. Within eight months, we found a slightly cheaper flat on rent, and we moved to that flat, which was meant for the middle-income group. For a couple of years, we stayed in rented houses. However, purchasing my home was a dream for us. One day, a builder named Pranlal Fultaria came to the office of Mr. S.I. Nanavati for some legal case-related work. Coincidentally, my senior told me to handle his case and take case details from him. During the discussion, he revealed that he was launching a new scheme near judges' bungalows in the Bodakdev area of Ahmedabad. I told him that I wanted my own house but I had no money. He said that he would not insist on a big upfront amount. On payment of a small amount, he booked my house in the proposed scheme. The price of the flat was six lakh twenty-five thousand rupees. I neither had enough funds to purchase the flat nor had taxable income to apply for a loan. So, I asked my brother Ashesh to lend his name for obtaining a loan because he was a Development Officer in Life Insurance Corporation having a fixed income. I purchased my first home with some contribution from my parents, obtaining a joint loan of Rs. 4 lakh from Gruh Finance, one lakh from my dear friend Mehul Sheth, fifty thousand rupees from my cousin Mihir Parikh, and twenty-five thousand rupees from my cousin Aashish Desai. Still, I was short of twenty-five thousand rupees and the amount required for purchasing furniture. I proposed a client named Dr. Jayen C. Shah to enter into a retainership agreement for two years to generate the required seventy-five thousand rupees. Dr. Jayen was staying abroad and he needed someone to look after his mailbox, pay rents, pay maintenance to his divorced wife and daughters, and other similar menial work, and occasionally give him legal advice. I proposed to him that I would do all these menial works for him and act as his attorney as well. I did the aforementioned works of collecting mails from his mailbox, paying rent to the old landlady in whose house Dr. Jayen had stored his excess furniture, etc., and other works dutifully for two years and justified the fee paid to me for the retainership agreement by Dr. Jayen. It is interesting to mention that for a bank loan, I needed two guarantors. In those days, looking at my income, it was difficult to find two persons who would stand as guarantors for me. I requested one of my distant relatives to be my guarantor, which he diplomatically refused. Rather than signing the guarantee form, he started giving me advice, saying that his senior had told him that one should never become a guarantor for any person. His senior's advice was that one should render help by giving cash if anyone is in need of it but not to become a guarantor of someone. My distant relative neither offered cash nor his signature on the guarantee form. In contrast, my two friends Anil Pandya and Maulik Shah signed the guarantee form without asking a single question as they had full faith not in my capacity to earn but in the honesty and integrity that I would not put them in any trouble. This is how our first home was made! We named our first home "Raseshwari," which was my mother's name who died just a few months before we moved to our new home. She could not see the first house of her son. Somehow, she had faith in me that I would someday be able to stand on my own legs. I stood on my own legs but with crutches in the form of a loan borrowed from my friends and cousins. I must mention that none of my friends or cousins ever reminded me to return the amount given to me for the purchase of my first home, but I returned them the amount in two years. I am indeed beholden to them for helping me in those days when no one was willing to have faith in my capabilities.

As you start earning more, your desires would also increase. When we had no home of our own, my wife and I desired that we would be happiest if we could purchase a house with even one bedroom, a kitchen, and a drawing room. But now having a home, I started thinking of buying a car. We purchased a Maruti Car, and I started feeling like a successful person. Later on, I bought an Opel Car in the false belief of creating a higher status in society. The car was a German brand which gave poor fuel average of 6 km per litre. The car turned out to be expensive, so I got it fitted with an LPG kit to save money! The original charm of the car was lost, but my status of possessing an expensive car remained with me.

Thereafter I purchased a three-bedroom flat in the year 2008 and a four-bedroom flat in the year 2018 for a better status. Those events are unimportant, and I would like to avoid them. But again, in the year 2024, somehow the prospects of buying a bungalow came to my doorstep. It was quite an expensive bungalow. My adventurous mind, without thinking anything, decided to buy the bungalow. I was short of a substantial amount to reach the price fixed for the bungalow. I told the seller of the bungalow that I would pay the amount before the 30th August without knowing how. Fortunately, I got sufficient income and could fulfil my commitment. Interestingly, I decided to sell my existing flat and promised the buyer to vacate my flat by a particular date thinking that the bungalow would be ready for shifting there by that time. It so happened that my bungalow was not ready for shifting, and I had to vacate my existing flat as per the promise to the buyer of my flat. I had to stay in a rented flat for one month before we shifted to our new bungalow. I can say that because of the blessing of my parents and the universe, I could buy properties without facing many difficulties even though my decisions were supremely unplanned and unsound. Most of us are not willing to change the area of the city where we have stayed with parents. But in our case, I and my family have changed our residence without reasons seven times in the same city as if we were changing clothes!

Chapter 13

Decided to Cut the Branch of Tree I Was Sitting

It was my dream to become a high court judge at an early age. Somehow, my overall actions during the career as a high court advocate were judgeship-driven. After complete introspection, I can confidently say that I was truthful to the court at all times and to my clients, which is considered to be one of the required qualities for judgeship. I would never try to mislead the court during my career. My degree of honesty and uprightness was far superior to that of many advocates. I consciously used the phrase "degree of honesty" because, like most lawyers and businessmen, I was not honest in discharging tax obligations fully. My legal knowledge was reasonably good. Fortunately, I could earn a very good reputation as a lawyer, an academician, and a scholar. Perhaps for the aforementioned reasons or because I was a partner to advocate Vijay Patel, my name started circulating among the high court lawyers as a prospective candidate for judgeship. Luckily, in 2009, I was invited by the then Chief Justice of Gujarat High Court, who asked me my wish whether I was willing to become a judge. I was more than keen to join the prestigious constitutional office of a high court judge and hence said an emphatic "YES". We, eight advocates, were invited to fill up the form in February 2009. The politics began from the day we filled up the form. One of the senior judges forming part of the high court collegium wanted one lady advocate to become a judge who was not part of the list of the recommended candidates, and similarly, another judge forming part of the collegium wanted one more advocate whose name was not recommended. The Chief Justice did not want to send more than eight names. In this internal battle among the members of the collegium of the high court, the names were not sent up until May 2009. Finally, it seems that a compromise was reached between the aforementioned two judges. The collegium decided to axe two names from the candidates who had filled up the forms in February 2009. The candidates other than the two to be axed were called again to sign the form. Instead of filling up the whole form again, only the last page of the form was changed, and we were asked to sign the last page again with the date of May 2009. I went to the secretary to the CJ and signed the last page again. Coincidentally, one of the names to be omitted was my cousin. During the recess time, I just asked my cousin whether he had been asked to sign the last page of the form again. He said that he was not asked to sign it again. So, all members of the Bar came to know by the next day that to accommodate the favourites of two senior judges, my cousin and the other advocate were made the scapegoats. Possibly these facts reached the Supreme Court also later on. The appointments were delayed for six months. In the meantime, a new list of the candidates from the subordinate judiciary was approved and sent to the Supreme Court. So, both the lists were merged after eight months to the best of my belief. The new list contained names of four judges from the subordinate judiciary. Out of the four, two were considered to be very close to the BJP government, the ruling party in Gujarat. There were all possibilities that their names would be dropped since the centre was ruled by Congress. Be that as it may, politics and personal relations with the CJI play a major role in any appointment or non-appointment. At last, after two years of the sending of the recommendations, only two were appointed from the first list of eight candidates. I have heard that the controversial judges of the subordinate court judiciary had a good rapport with the CJI, so everything seems to have been perfectly managed to see that their names were cleared by the centre. So, from the second list, all judges from the subordinate judiciary were appointed, but two of them with a condition that they would be transferred to any state other than Gujarat. They were actually transferred outside the State of Gujarat. After the BJP won the parliamentary election, both the judges were brought back to Gujarat. One of them is made a Supreme Court Judge too, out of turn.

In the year 2009, my book on "Writs and Constitutional Remedies" was released. In the year 2010, my revised edition of the book on law of contempt was also published. Besides the above-mentioned achievements, I was always considered to be an honest and hardworking advocate. So, I was confident that there should not be any obstacle in my becoming a judge. However, I did not realise that I was a partner to a person closely attached to the Bhartiya Janta Party. At that time, in the central government, the ruling party was Congress-led coalition. It is my firm belief that once your name is proposed for a judgeship, you must meet all powerful persons who have some say in the matter of appointment if you really want to get an appointment. Being confident of my merit, I chose not to meet a very influential advocate who was a part of the Congress party and who was practising in the Supreme Court. I was branded as a BJP candidate to the Supreme Court collegium through the Ministry of Law and Justice. I did not meet any of the judges forming part of the collegium. The Chief Justice who recommended my name was by that time elevated as a judge of the Supreme Court. I thought the collegium would ask the said judge if they had any query about my suitability. But my expectations and faith in the collegium were belied by the aforesaid final decision of the collegium. I came to know that my name had been omitted only when other proposed judges' names were cleared and they came to be appointed in the month of February 2011. It took two years to take the final decision on the eight names proposed by the high court collegium for judgeship. It seems that my name was dropped only for political reasons. It is my firm belief that your choices in life play an important role in creating your destiny. When I exercised my choice of becoming a partner to Mr. Vijay Patel, my destiny was also decided favourably and unfavourably. I became standing counsel and a successful lawyer because of Mr. Vijay Patel. My name was perhaps started circulating for judgeship partly due to my being a partner to Mr. Vijay Patel. I doubt that it was sent because of my own competence. On my own competence, it would have been sent but not at my age of 44 but maybe at the age of 50 or 51. My name was dropped for this very reason that I was a partner to Mr. Vijay Patel. I tried to find out the correct reason for dropping my name from the list of proposed judges, but I have no clue as to why it was omitted. I received a clue from some sources after two years that the central government raised an objection against my name as I was a partner to Vijay Patel, a BJP MP/MLA. It is a convention that when an objection is raised against any candidate, the names are sent back to the high court for reconsideration. Since the Chief Justice was changed by the time names were sent back to the high court for reconsideration, the new Chief Justice had a major role to play in reiterating my name. I never met the new Chief Justice for recommending my name again. The Chief Justice had close connections with the Supreme Court lawyer belonging to the Congress party, and the Chief Justice was wedded to the Congress philosophy. The Chief Justice was in a hurry to become a Supreme Court Judge, so at the instance of the aforesaid Supreme Court lawyer, he omitted my name. The said Chief Justice became a Supreme Court Judge very quickly by climbing on the shoulders of the aforesaid Supreme Court lawyer who was very influential in the Congress government and in the decision-making process.

I completely lost faith in the collegium system of appointment. I was disheartened and dejected by the entire episode. I started pondering over the collegium system and guessing the reasons that might have resulted in the omission of my name from the list of the recommended advocates for judgeship. I found that in the entire selection process no explanation is asked from the candidate concerned against the adverse material put up before all the authorities involved in the decision-making process. Even a courtesy letter is not sent that the recommendation has resulted in non-appointment. I also explored the possibility of justiciability of the decision of the collegium system in the court of law. After pondering over the issue for six months and doing research on the topic, I jotted down certain constitutional and legal issues that can be argued if I decided to challenge the omission of my name. I read the Supreme Court's landmark judgements in S. P. Gupta's case, Supreme Court AOR's case, Presidential Reference's judgement, and other relevant judgements thoroughly. I could find out many arguable points for questioning the decision of the collegium. Basically, the arguable issues were viz. my right to know the reasons for non-appointment, whether I had any say in respect of the adverse material relied upon by the authorities, whether all authorities involved in the decision-making process were consulted on the material used against me, whether the suitability of a recommended candidate is possible to be judicially reviewed. Whether I should challenge the collegium system of appointment was mainly influenced by the decision of the Supreme Court in Sankalchand Himmatlal Sheth's case where a high court judge challenged his transfer from Gujarat High Court to Andhra Pradesh high court and the Supreme Court laid down the law relating to the transfer of a high court judge. Secondly, the S.P. Gupta's case was also pertaining to the non-extension of the terms of three additional judges and also pertaining to the transfer of some judges of high courts. So, I thought that if I challenged the decision of the collegium, it would be in the larger interest of all concerned. The court will have to decide the constitutional issues that would be raised and it would prevent injustice to the candidates whose names would be recommended in the future from being treated unfairly. With this pious intention, I finally decided to challenge the existing flaws in the collegium system of appointment of judges. I knew very well that if I choose to challenge the decision of the collegium, I would be foreclosing my doors for judgeship for all time to come. But I was ready to sacrifice my personal interest for the larger good. First of all, I expressed my wish to challenge the omission of my name and my intention to question the collegium system to a limited extent to my friend advocate Percy Kavina. I discussed all the points I had researched for the past six months and convinced him that it is possible to question the collegium system on limited grounds. We then discussed my intention to file a petition with Senior Advocate Mr. Mihir Thakore and persuaded him to argue my case. Initially, there was reluctance on his part as he was of the view that it may not yield the desired result but after careful examination of the points to be raised in the petition and my obstinacy, he agreed to argue my case pro bono. I just wanted to know the reasons for the omission of my name. I made it clear to him that I do not want an appointment or reconsideration of my name but want reforms in the collegium system of appointment. He was authorised to make such a statement before the bench so that the court would be willing to examine the larger issues raised in the petition. This was also stated in the petition also if I remember correctly. Moreover, the matter was likely to be listed before the Acting Chief Justice's bench which I trusted a lot. However, as soon as the petition was filed in the registry, the people became aware of the filing of such a unique petition. The message reached the Acting Chief Justice too. The Acting Chief Justice was my well-wisher so he was surprised or maybe shocked by the filing of the petition by me. He immediately sent a message to me to meet him at his home. I obeyed his message and reached his home. He warmly welcomed and tried to convince me not to proceed with the petition and withdraw it. He asked me who was behind me to goad me to file such a petition. I politely answered that it was solely my decision and I could never be pressurised or persuaded by anyone to do a particular thing in my life. He said that it would mar my future prospects to become a high court judge. But I was blind and bubbling with enthusiasm to bring reforms in the collegium system. He got disappointed with my immaturity and blind faith in the impartiality of the justice delivery system. Finally, he gave up and expressed his best wishes to me.

The petition was listed before his bench as per the roster two days after my meeting with him. The Acting Chief Justice recused himself from the bench as he had interacted with me in private. All the lawyers were surprised by the decision of the Acting Chief Justice to recuse himself. People asked me questions about the recusal, but I did not say anything about my private meeting with the Acting Chief Justice. If the 1st court refuses to hear a particular case, ordinarily it would be listed before the next senior judge's bench. The next senior judge also had high regard for me and was an old acquaintance, being an advocate elevated from the Bar. It appears that some politics were played in listing my matter. As said earlier, the previous Chief Justice who had to reconsider my name had been elevated as a Supreme Court Judge by the time all these events happened. Perhaps, the said judge played an important role in placing my case before the fourth senior judge's bench, who also had Congress moorings. The second judge who was to sit with him was one of the candidates whose name was recommended with mine. In my petition, one of the prayers was to produce the file before the court pertaining to my recommendation. I was of the belief that the second judge would recuse himself from the hearing of my case as it would have caused some embarrassment to him if the entire file was placed before the court. However, he did not recuse from the case. It appears that the action plan was pre-decided not to issue even a notice in such an important case. It was to be nipped in the bud. If a notice was issued and the file had been placed before the court, it would have caused embarrassment to the central government and the ruling party there. I was sure that there was nothing against me, and therefore I dared to question the decision of the collegium. If any false reason is found on the file, the legal fraternity knew me and my credentials very well, and they would believe that it must be a concocted reason. The entire bar was curious to know the outcome of the case. The courtroom was fully packed with lawyers, and my case was called out for hearing. The judges presiding on the bench were very angry from the beginning. Their anger was quite visible from their faces and body language. In fifteen minutes, the petition was summarily dismissed. We all got shocked as we expected the court to issue notice to the respondents to justify their action. Thus, I permanently closed the door to becoming a high court judge. This reminds me of the story of Kavi Kalidas (a Sanskrit poet of old times) cutting the same branch of a tree where he was sitting. I had two options: one was to bear the injustice silently and wait for the recommendation of my name again, and the second was to challenge the collegium system for the larger benefit of all stakeholders. In either case, there were possibilities of repenting my action in the future. I considered my rejection as an opportunity to bring reforms in the system and chose the path of challenging the decision of the collegium. Today, when I see the candidates, whose names were recommended with mine as sitting Supreme Court Judges or occupying the seat of a Chief Justice, it pains me a little bit. If had tolerated the injustice of dropping my name, my name would have been definitely recommended second time in a year or two. At the same time, I feel grateful to the destiny for making me a Senior

Advocate having full freedom without any inhibition associated with judgeship. Perhaps, considering my rebellious nature of not going by dogmas, and being a proponent of lateral thinking, destiny thought it fit not to suffocate me in the disciplined career of judgeship. Today I have a mixed feeling of repentance for not becoming a high court judge who had all potentials to become a Supreme Court judge and joy of being a free advocate. The judge who dismissed my petition coincidentally became the victim of the collegium system when the BJP was in power. He was transferred from one high court to another and not made a Chief Justice of any high court despite his seniority. I still supported that judge by signing the resolution passed by the Gujarat High Court Advocates' Association since my fight was against certain flaws in the collegium system and politics predominating in the system. I was the Vice President of the Gujarat High Court Advocates' Association at that time, and the paradox was that I was invited to speak by the Bar Association of the high court where the aforesaid judge was last posted, to speak on the political interference in appointments and transfers of judges.

Undaunted by the rejection of my petition by the Gujarat High Court, I decided to file a petition before the Supreme Court to challenge the decision of the high court. I must admit that because of not managing the litigation in the Supreme Court properly, I faced defeat in the Supreme Court also. For Supreme Court cases, I usually engage an advocate on record who was most competent and smart in managing the filing. Somehow, he showed disinclination in filing my case. It would have been easier for me if he had agreed to file the case in the Supreme Court as he had very good relations with all designated Senior Advocates and most of the judges. I had to opt for an advocate who was comparatively new. We thought of engaging a Senior Advocate and explored various options. Finally, we decided on one name. We had a conference with the aforesaid Senior Advocates who is considered to be one of the best advocates in the Supreme Court and persuaded him to argue my case. He agreed to take up my case. But when my case was listed for admission hearing in the Supreme Court, the Senior Advocate did not turn up. The bench of justice Aftab Alam and Ranjana Desai admonished the AOR, saying that he should avoid filing such a petition and asked him to withdraw the petition. I was present in the court but I could not speak since I was a litigant represented through an advocate. My petition was dismissed summarily. I lost both the future chance of being recommended for judgeship again and my dream to bring reforms in the current system of appointment of high court judges. It is a matter of coincidence that the Senior Advocate who did not turn up was directly recommended for being appointed as a Supreme Court Judge. His candidature was rejected because of political interference since he had represented the Congress government in all important cases when the Congress was ruling the nation. He was a Solicitor General or Additional Solicitor General during the Congress rule and perhaps he was wedded to the Congress philosophy. By his non-appointment, the Senior Advocate lost nothing but the nation was deprived of a very competent Supreme Court Judge.

Chapter 14

Unsuccessful Challenge to the System of Designating Senior Advocates

Somewhere in the year 2015, I applied to be designated as a Senior Advocate. At that time, the high court had already enacted the Rules (2012 Rules) for designating Senior Advocates. One of the Rules required that an advocate applying to be designated as a Senior Advocate should have a net taxable income of rupees fifteen lakh in the preceding three years. Net taxable income of rupees fifteen lakh would mean gross income from the profession should be more than rupees twenty-five lakhs at least. I had an aggregate net taxable income of rupees forty-eight lakhs in the last preceding three years. In substance, I was meeting the average rupees fifteen lakh net taxable income criterion. The Rule provided the power to relax this requirement in a particular case by the full court. I had to my credit the achievement of being the author of five law books. I had written many articles in law journals of good repute. I had worked as an Additional Standing Counsel for the Central government for six years. Moreover, I was found suitable to be recommended for a high court judge's post in the year 2009. Besides all the above feathers in my cap, I had a good reputation among judges and members of the Bar. So, I thought that there should not be any difficulty in getting the designation of Senior Advocate. I, therefore, took a decision to apply for the designation of Senior Advocate. To my dismay, my application was not put up for consideration at all as I was not meeting the income criterion according to the committee involved in the decision-making process. In my application itself, I had stated that in the event of a narrow interpretation of the Rule prescribing income criterion, my case for relaxing the income criterion may be considered. I got disheartened by the pedantic interpretation of the income Rule by the decision-makers. I consulted one of the judges to find out whether on the aspect of granting relaxation to me from the income criterion all judges were consulted or not. He said that no such request for relaxation was put up for consideration before the full court. He was of the view that once the power to grant designation was vested under the 2012 Rules with the full court, the power of relaxation could not be exercised by two or three senior judges only. Emboldened by the aforesaid interpretation of the Rule by one of the judges, I decided to request the full court to consider my application for exemption from the income criterion. However, it seems that the application was not put up before the full court, and I was conveyed by the Registrar General that the application for exemption was regretted. I got really furious about this but kept silent this time. Unlike challenging the decision, I decided to bear the injustice meted out to me. Thus, I took out the sword from the scabbard but having learnt one lesson of unsuccessfully challenging the collegium system of appointment of judges, I immediately put back the sword in the scabbard. I did not challenge the decision this time but only asked the full court to simply consider my application for exemption, which was turned down. I must mention that I was equipped with the decision of the Delhi High Court, which had held the income criterion in the matter of designation of Senior Advocate to be unconstitutional. But I did not press that decision of the Delhi High Court into service to question the decision of the court not to put up my application for consideration on the ground of lack of eligibility. This time I decided first to enter the elite club of Senior Advocates and then raise my voice against the system.

After failing to get my application for exemption considered, I decided to study the origin and historical aspects of the system of designation and how it was introduced in India. My research went on for a considerable amount of time. I found that the current system of designating Senior Advocates had been derived from the English system of designating an advocate to be a Queen's Counsel or King's Counsel. In India, prior to the Constitution of India and the Advocates Act, 1961, there was no system of a court designating an advocate to be a Senior Advocate. The system of recognising an advocate to be a Senior Advocate was evolved by the Bombay Bar Association (Original Side) on a purely voluntary and non-discriminatory basis. The voluntary system recognising an advocate to be a Senior Advocate got distorted from the year 1954 when the newly established Supreme Court of India amended the practice of voluntary recognition of an advocate to be a Senior Advocate by transferring the power to the court from the Bar Association. Thereafter, the 1st Law Commission of India, in its 14th Report, without examining the practice of designating an advocate to be a Senior Advocate on the touchstone of articles 14, 18, and 21 of the Constitution of India, recommended continuing the court-conferred system of designation which was introduced by the Supreme Court in its Rules just six years prior. I found no rationale for introducing or continuing the system of designation as the Law Commission itself accepts in its 14th Report that it is based on the Queen's Counsel System of England, which had no rationale. In England, a hierarchical society is an accepted norm, and there a title, honour, or distinction can be conferred by the crown. In India, our constitution prohibits the conferment of all distinctions, honours, or titles except educational and military distinctions. Be that as it may, I do not want to trouble the readers with the points of arguments against the constitutionality of Section 16 of the Advocates Act, 1961, which provides for designating an advocate to be a Senior Advocate in this book.

However, before I entered the elite class of Senior Advocates, an opportunity arose to question the constitutionality of Section 16 of the Advocates Act, 1961 when I became President of the Gujarat High Court Advocates' Association. However, I miserably failed in my challenge before the Supreme Court of India. These details of how I challenged the constitutional validity before the Supreme court are stated in the next chapter as the same pertains to my acts partly as the President of the Bar Association.

Chapter 15

Removed From the Post of President of the Bar Association and Failing in Bar Council Election

In the year 2016-17, I contested the election for the post of President of the Gujarat High Court Advocates' Association (hereafter GHCAA). In that year, I had already decided to contest for the post of President of GHCAA as I had been working as the Vice President of the GHCAA for one or two terms. However, when nominations were finalised, I found that Mr. Vijay Patel, my ex-partner, had decided to contest against me. I did not understand his move of filing a nomination as he had been an MP and MLA for three terms, and this post was a very small post for his stature. I was asked not to contest the election for the post of President by a few lawyers, saying that Mr. Vijay Patel had a good political background and that once upon a time I was his partner. However, since I was holding the post of Vice President for two terms, I did not budge from my decision to go higher. Anyway, I won the election, but it was not joyful. I did not like the defeat of my ex-partner Vijay Patel, with whom I had worked for long seventeen years, and my success in the profession was substantially because of him. As the President of the GHCAA, I could serve the Bar to the best of my ability and with the satisfaction of most of the members of the Bar. Senior Advocate Mr. Dushyant Dave, Advocate Mr. S. I Nanavati, Senior Advocate Mr. K.G. Vakharia, Senior Advocate Mr. Shirish Sanjanwala, Senior Advocate Mihir Thakore, Senior Advocate Mr. K. S. Nanavati,

Senior Advocate Mr. Yatin Oza, and many other advocates, without my asking for donation, donated approximately fifty lakh rupees just in the first six months of my assuming as the President of GHCAA. This amount was used for creating better infrastructure for the members of the Bar. I would not like to burden the book with all my achievements as the President of the Bar, since this book is not the right place to project those achievements as President of GHCAA. However, some important things that happened during my tenure are stated in the later part of this chapter.

Coming back to my views against the system of designating Senior Advocates, I would like to inform that somehow as it was destined, an opportunity to challenge the system of designating Senior Advocates surfaced when I came to know about Indira Jaising's petition which had questioned the system of designating Senior Advocate on the ground of opaqueness and lack of objectivity. I persuaded my managing committee to file an intervention petition and question the constitutional validity of Section 16 of the Advocates Act, 1961 since many lawyers had faced rejection for being designated as Senior Advocate. Many deserving advocates were denied the designation and it had created a great heartburning to them but they were not willing to examine the rationale of the system. A notice of intention of our Association to intervene in the matter of Indira Jaising was pasted in red ink with bold letters at all conspicuous places seeking responses from the members of our Association on this important issue. As what normally happens nobody reads any Notice of GHCAA, no objection was received and we filed an intervention application in Supreme Court. I decided to appear on behalf of the GHCAA in the intervention application before the Supreme Court of India. When the matter was listed before the Supreme Court of India, I was thorough with my research and preparation. I got up for arguments. The bench consisting of Justice Gogoi, Justice Nariman and justice

Navin Sinha was little unwilling to allow me a detailed audience. But, after hearing me for the initial five minutes the bench was curious to hear me on the subject. The bench allowed me to argue for one hour and ten minutes approximately to make my points good. I had full trust in the bench more particularly one of the members of the Bench was Mr. Nariman. I expected that Justice Nariman would write the judgement but it was Justice Gogoi who wrote the judgement. My one hour arguments were recorded in one small paragraph and dealt with perfunctorily. An absurd simile was given to compare the system of designation with senior bureaucrats and senior Docters Doctors. I was again disappointed with the manner in which my arguments were dealt with by the bench. Besides the fact that arguments were not dealt with appropriately my name was recorded as advocate Ashim Anand instead of Asim Pandya in the judgement. In my personal view, the judgement is constitutionally unsustainable. The entire judgement would fall down by reading the first line of paragraph 11 which states that why the Queen's Counsel was introduced in England or what was the rationale of the system is not discernible from the history. To my mind how can something which has no rationale be allowed to continue in India! Anyway, we lost our battle or you can say my battle on behalf of general advocates including myself whose application was not put up for consideration on the ground of the income criterion.

During this period, there came the Law Commission's 266th Report recommending many far-reaching changes in the Advocates Act, 1961 adverse to the lawyer community. This report was given pursuant to the judgement of the Supreme Court in Mahipal Singh Rana's case. The report of the Law Commission resulted in large-scale protest all over India. The Bar Council of India called an urgent meeting of the Presidents of all High Courts in Delhi. I was also invited to Delhi by BCI. I made a detailed study of the recommendations made by the Law Commission of India in the 266th Report. In my view, in

Mahipal Singh Rana's case, the Supreme Court had overstepped its constitutional limit and almost directed Parliament to amend the Advocates Act, 1961. I was given an opportunity to express my views by BCI, and I made many suggestions, including filing a review application in Mahipal Singh Rana's case. My speech was liked by the BCI chairman and all office bearers of the BCI. The BCI constituted an internal committee to examine the 266th Report and make counter suggestions. I was inducted as a member of the internal committee of the BCI. We made several suggestions, including the abolition of Section 16 of the Advocates Act, 1961. I filed a review petition on behalf of the GHCAA in the matter of *Mahipal Singh Rana's* case. The review petition is still pending. Fortunately, the draconian recommendations of the Law Commission in its 266th Report have remained on the file only in the light of the widespread protest made by lawyers all over India.

During the second year of my term as the President of GHCAA, dirty petty politics started showing its presence. Many advocates were envied by my sudden rise and important decisions taken by me for the benefit of the members of the Bar. One day, the news was flashed that an advocate was murdered in Jamnagar. It was not clear whether he was murdered for personal reasons or for discharging his duties as an advocate. To my knowledge, it was for some personal reasons unconnected with his duties as a lawyer that had resulted in his murder. Some members requested me to call for an urgent meeting of the GHCAA and to go on strike. At that time, the Supreme Court had ruled in its decision in the case of *Krishnakant Tamarakar* that lawyers should not resort to strikes and boycotts. The judgement further says that if any association resorts to a strike, the office bearers would be held responsible for contempt. The meeting of the GHCAA was called where the members demanded that we should go on strike to show solidarity to the murdered lawyer. I drew the attention of the members of the GHCAA to the judgement of the Supreme Court in *Krishnakant Tamarakar's* case and refused to resort to a strike. I was not afraid of the possible contempt action but I was of the view that if an advocate is murdered for a reason unconnected with the discharge of his duties, there was no need to resort to a strike or boycott. It seems that it was a pre-decided plan of some advocates that I would refuse to go on strike and the members would pass a vote of no confidence against me. The meeting went unruly, and I closed the proceeding of the meeting and left the meeting hall. However, some forty lawyers, after my leaving the meeting, continued the meeting and illegally passed a vote of no confidence against me. The news started circulating that I was deposed from the post. I could have stuck to the post, but I chose the legal path of challenging the aforesaid "no confidence motion" and my illegal removal by forty to fifty lawyers by filing a petition in the High Court of Gujarat. While the said petition was pending, finally, a secret ballot voting was done at the instance of the group of advocates supporting me on whether I should continue as the President of the Bar. By a thumping majority, I was reinstated to the post of President of GHCAA. However, by the time I was restored to the post of President, I had lost all interest in the post. Within one week of my restoration, I resigned from the post with dignity.

In the high court Building, there was no full-fledged canteen for lawyers. So, during my tenure as the President of GHCAA, I took the initiative to renovate the canteen area and to get a well-reputed contractor to run a canteen for lawyers. The look of the canteen was completely changed to befit the stature of lawyers. Due to the new contractor, we had to retrench four employees of the GHCAA. There was tremendous resistance from a very small but notorious segment of the Bar. They instigated old employees and other members to ensure that the new contractor could not run the canteen. They brought unbearable pressure on me to change my decision and take those four employees into service. I did not succumb to the pressure. If those four employees were reinstated, they would not allow the contractor to run the canteen at the instance of the notorious groups of advocates. Though all four employees were eligible to get one lakh or one lakh twenty-five thousand towards the retrenchment compensation on the assumed applicability of the labour laws. But because of the pressure brought by the aforesaid small segment of advocates, each one was given four lakh fifty thousand as compensation for leaving their job. For this, I did not use the fund of the association but requested some Senior Advocates viz. Senior Advocate S. I. Nanavati, Senior Advocate Shirish Sanjanwala, Senior Advocate K S Nanavati, Senior Advocate Mihir Thakor, Senior Advocate Yatin Oza, who extended help to me to overcome the issue. I am thankful to all those Senior Advocates for helping me create an exclusive canteen for lawyers with a good ambience and run the canteen through a reputed contractor.

Our Association was though functioning for more than fifty years, it had no Section 80G registration under the Income Tax Act. But I and my team did it.

I noticed that for the election for the post of Member of the Bar Council of Gujarat, the advocates from the high court were not willing to go to the city court for casting their votes as it was the only polling booth available to all lawyers. During my tenure, I filed a petition and argued that the right to vote means the right to vote at the most convenient place nearby the GHCAA. Otherwise, it was not a right at all. The court ruled in favour of GHCAA, and the polling booth was given in the high court premises after more than fifty-five years of the establishment of the Gujarat High Court. I was happy to be part of this victory.

The sudden success as the President of GHCAA emboldened me to contest the Bar Council of Gujarat (hereafter BCG) election.

Considering my stature, my aforementioned contribution to the development of a robust Bar, and my work in the field of academics, I was of the belief that winning the election would be a cakewalk. But I was wrong. I travelled all over Gujarat and met the members of district and taluka level Bars. I understood their difficulties and problems. I received a great welcome everywhere that strengthened my belief that I would easily win the BCG election. However, the election result belied my expectations. I realised that the BCG election is fought in a different manner and with different parameters. It requires offering dinners at all taluka and district Bars to the members of the Bar. A candidate contesting the BCG election has to provide air conditioning or other such facilities to the members of the Bar. I did none of those things that matter for winning the BCG election. I just spent on petrol expenses for travelling all over Gujarat, getting printed pamphlets delineating my contributions and other achievements, and using social media through a professional. Finally, when the results were out, I was eliminated in the 40th position out of the total twenty-five candidates to be elected by single transferable vote of proportionate representation. I realised that I was an absolute misfit for such an election. It was a lesson for me. I decided not to contest the BCG election in the future.

Be that as it may, I learnt many lessons by occupying the office of the President of GHCAA, contesting BCG elections, and becoming more mature in my own eyes.

Chapter 16

Entered the Elite Class of Senior Advocates to Avoid Feeling of Discrimination

In the judgement of the Supreme Court in *Indiara Jaising's* case, the income criterion was omitted, and all high courts were directed to frame the Rules for Designation of Senior Advocates in tune with the final directions given by the Supreme Court. By the time the aforementioned judgement of the Supreme Court omitted the income criterion, my income had also increased substantially, crossing the threshold limit under the 2012 Rules (Old Rules). Now the Supreme Court had laid down objective criteria and provided for interaction with the candidate applying for the designation. I had a distinct advantage of being ahead in the race over the other applicants due to having written five law books and many articles in law journals. I was sure that I would get 15 marks extra for the above academic achievements over other candidates. Most importantly, the committee for designation consisted of the Acting Chief Justice and two other senior most judges who had a favourable opinion of me. I still believe that I was lucky to have been designated as a Senior Advocate, not that I did not deserve it, but due to the occurrences of all favourable factors simultaneously. I express my gratitude to the Designation committee consisting of the Acting Chief Justice Mr. Anant S. Dave, justice S.R. Brahmbhatt, justice Ms. H.N. Devani, Senior Advocate Mr. S.N. Shelat, and Advocate General Mr. Kamal Trivedi who found me worthy of the Senior Advocate's designation.

As said earlier, I was keen to become a Senior Advocate for the reason that if a Senior Advocate himself protests against the system, it makes a huge difference. Otherwise, one can be easily branded as a disgruntled advocate not made a Senior Advocate is protesting the system. Secondly, I had constant feelings of being discriminated when I was not a designated as Senior Advocate and I did not want to face this discrimination throughout my life. These are two reasons why I chose to apply for designation. I know that all general advocates have a feeling of being discriminated by creating a class within the class. I was no exception to it.But some members of the Bar were and are of the view I should not have applied at all if I was against the system. Anyway, you will find people criticising whatever you do. I have learnt to ignore such people and decided to follow what I believed to be the right course of action. Let me inform you all that even after I was made a Senior Advocate, I continued my fight against the system of designation which lacks any rationale. I wrote letters to the Prime Minister, Law Minister and Chief Justice to abolish the system of designation and omit Section 16 of the Advocates Act, 1961. When the Prime Minister abolished read beacons from the cars of all dignitaries, I compared the class of Senior Advocate as the red beacon of the profession and urged the Prime Minister to end the said practice and bring equality among the advocates. I even filed one petition in the Supreme Court through some advocates from different districts of the State of Gujarat that either the system should be abolished or the designation system should percolate in the districts and taluka level courts also. The current system has no mechanism to designate trial court advocates as Senior Advocate. The Supreme Court dismissed my petition on the ground that it was premature and I should approach the high court when the actual cause of action arises. My argument that the current system is based on certain objective and certain subjective criteria that are not possible to be fulfilled by a trial court lawyer was simply brushed aside by the Supreme Court. Prior to the aforesaid petition, there was not a single lawyer of a trial court who was designated as a Senior Advocate. In the State of Gujarat just in the last three years, three advocates of Ahmedabad City Civil Court who were influential were designated as Senior Advocates. I may not be misunderstood to label these three advocates as incompetent. They may be competent but they had special factors in their favour which other trial court lawyers do not have. Two were very close to a Supreme Court Judge and the third one had never practised litigation. Even after being designated, he has not appeared in the high court in a single case. The current system is based on objective criteria of the standing in the profession of an applicant, the reported judgements to the credit of an applicant, his contribution in the field of law and thirty-five percent on *ipse dixit* of the committee. There is no system that if an applicant scores a particular percentage of marks, he would be designated as a Senior Advocate. So, today also it substantially depends on the discretion or I dare say whims and caprice of the committee for designation who is to be designated as a Senior Advocate. The objective criteria hardly play any role in the matter of designation. They are simply illusions created to justify the constitutional validity of the practice of designation.

Since I am opposed to the division of advocates into Senior Advocates and general advocates, I have stopped using this designation on my files, my court bags, my office premises, in the foyer of the office building etc. I have some visiting cards and letterheads with my designation printed on them which I propose to discontinue after they are exhausted. I have only once used the special privilege conferred upon a Senior Advocate under Section 23 of the Advocates Act, 1961 where some lawyers in an important case wanted to show their superiority by arguing first over my standing and seniority at the Bar. I pressed into service Section 23 at the beginning of the hearing and all other lawyers who wanted to begin arguments were stunned by my unexpected explosion. Barring this incident, I had never tried to use the tag of a Senior Advocate anywhere. In the court proceeding also I am not bothered whether I am addressed as a Senior Advocate or not or whether the judgement reflects my name with the designation Senior Advocate. I am happy that I am not being discriminated in court proceedings and precincts anymore. I just wanted to maintain my dignity based on my knowledge of law, my academic contribution in the field of law, and the standing at the Bar with huge experience of handling all types of cases. The general perception among the judges, lawyers and litigants is that if a person is not a Senior Advocate, all his achievements and contributions are of no consequence. Recently the Supreme Court and some high courts have granted this designation generously to many persons. The granting of this designation to many advocates has the same effect of obliterating the distinction. I am happy that it has reduced the importance of a handful of designated Senior Advocates. I hope that a day will come when this division of advocates into two classes will be brought to an end, and I will be the happiest person when that happens. I learned in the first week of March 2025 that the Supreme Court is re-examining the process of designation to a limited extent. Again, I seized the opportunity and wrote a fourteen-point letter to the President of our Bar association requesting him to intervene by filing an application in the pending matter before the Supreme Court of India. I sent the aforesaid open letter to Live Law, Bar & Bench and other electronic platforms/ law journals/news agencies with a hope that it would be published. In my view these fourteen points mentioned in the open letter cover everything about Section 16 of the Advocates Act, 1961, its history in India, its legality and constitutionality. But to my misfortune, neither our Bar association nor the aforesaid media platforms published it. My efforts did not yield the desired result.

Let us hope the Supreme Court someday examines afresh the legality and validity of the process and makes it at least non-discriminatory if it does not declare Section 16 of the Advocates Act, 1961 unconstitutional. I have made and will continue to make every effort to see that this discriminatory system is abolished or it is completely based on all objective criteria only so that it becomes non-discriminatory.

Chapter 17

Compelled to Resign From the Post of President of the Bar Again

I was not keen to contest the election again for the post of President because of certain bad experiences I had encountered in discharging my duties as the President of the Gujarat High Court Bar Association. Moreover, after winning election for the post of the President's, he is required to face dirty politics of the bar. I already had one such experience as the President of the Bar. Moreover, when duty as the President of the Bar is to be discharged sincerely, it demands spending at least three hours every day to resolve the issues of the members, for calling meetings of the Executive committee, calling extraordinary general body meetings, asking appointment with the Chief Justice, drafting the agenda and resolutions. Drafting of agenda, writing the minutes, resolutions, notices etc. were the works of the General Secretary but those works I had to perform because of the limitations of the General Secretary who had been elected during my tenure. Additionally, I was required to contribute to the coffer of the Bar for every function. I was of the belief that if I were to demand donations from the members of the Bar, I should also contribute. The post of President was quite taxing to me as it affected the time to be devoted to my practice and my family. These were the reasons that dissuaded me from contesting the election again.

However, because of the insistence of my friends and well-wishers, I decided to contest the election again in the year 2021 for the post of President as the members of the Bar believed that the other two candidates were not good for the larger interest of the Bar. I put up a condition to my friends and well-wishers who insisted on me to contest the election that I would not do my canvassing or election campaign and would not go to each voter seeking his or her vote. I also proposed that for the post of President, no canvassing or election campaign should be allowed since the Bar consisted of hardly two thousand members and therefore the candidate for the President's post should be such that every member knows him and his worth. Since I was not willing to contest the election out of my own desire and being a proponent of the "No canvassing" theory, I took the risk of practising the theory of "no canvassing" and "no election campaign" in the election for the post of President. My opponents got excited to know that I was not going to do canvassing. Many friends and well-wishers advised me that I should give up my obstinacy of sticking to my decision of no canvassing. But I stuck to what I had already declared publicly. Despite my weird decision of "not to canvass", I got elected as the President of GHAA again. I would give credit for my victory to Senior Advocate Mr. Yatin Oza who, without my requesting him to canvass for my candidature, relentlessly requested voters to vote for me, disregarding my foolishness of no campaigning. Our Chief Justice Mr. Aravind Kumar was surprised to know this kind of strange victory of mine. He said that in Karnataka for the Bar election, a candidate contesting for the post of President or Secretary usually spends more than fifty lakh rupees. When he asked me what amount I had spent on my election, my answer was "Zero". I even avoided canvassing through telephone or mobile! I just sent one message at the time of filing my nomination form that I had decided not to run an election campaign for myself as I had full trust in the wisdom of the members of the Bar. I said that the aforesaid message was the first and last message for my election campaign for the post of President. I simply urged the voters to exercise their discretion wisely at the time of voting. I said that it was not my ego not to reach everyone and ask for the vote but the futility of reaching everyone when all know me well. I made a general but fervent appeal to vote for me only once through a WhatsApp message. My personal view was and is that where the Bar consists of two thousand members and all of them know the contesting candidates very well, the election campaign is not to be encouraged, particularly when the voters possess a law degree and are considered to be the most learnt people. I think a practice should be evolved to arrange a short debate in the Bar room for the candidates contesting the post of President, Vice President and General Secretary where such candidates can appeal to the voters to cast their votes in his or her favour giving reasons why he is the best candidate for the post he is contesting.

During my stint as the President of Bar for the second time, one day in the court of the Chief Justice, a litigant said that he would like to argue his case in Gujarati as he did not know English. The Chief Justice insulted the litigant and stated that the official language of the court is English only. This incident drew the attention of the media and was widely published. Suddenly, a thought came to my mind that after seventy-five years of India's independence from British rule, why should there be a prohibition on speaking one's mother tongue in court proceedings? When every one of us knows our mother tongue, why should court proceedings continue in English only? After some days of the incident, there was a felicitation function for some judges of our court who had been elevated as Supreme Court Judges. I had decided to deliver my speech for the function in English, but at the last moment, I thought that since the whole audience knows Gujarati, why should I speak in English? I gave my speech in Gujarati, which was liked by many and disliked by some. I started researching this issue about permitting a regional language in high court proceedings. I found the answer in Article 348 of the Constitution of India. I wrote a letter to the Governor to issue authorisation under Article 348(2) of the

Constitution of India. This led to widespread protest in the high court Bar. Subordinate court Bars and the Bar Council of Gujarat supported my move. All advocates, including many Senior Advocates, pressured me to withdraw the letter which I had written in my capacity as the President of GHCAA without calling a general body meeting. I realised my mistake of writing a letter in my capacity as the President of the Bar without trying to ascertain the wish of the members of GHCAA and putting it before the managing committee. I, therefore, withdrew the letter but immediately wrote a letter in my individual capacity. This was also not approved by many. Their view was that once I am holding the position of the President of the Bar, my personal views would be imbued with the office I held. Hence, I decided to resign from the post, which was almost like removal from the office. But I decided to continue my movement for Gujarati. Fortunately, after my resignation, one person named Rohit Patel with one advocate came to me and expressed his desire to file a Public Interest Litigation for allowing Gujarati in the Gujarat High Court as a medium of expression. I was looking for such a person, and he came. After deep research, we came to know that the Governor of Gujarat (upon the advice of the council of ministers) had already issued such an authorisation in the year 2012. We filed a petition for implementing the authorisation already issued by the Governor in the year 2012 under Article 348(2). The judges and high court advocates all seemed to be against my petition. In such an important petition, the high court did not issue notice for one long year and later summarily dismissed the petition without dealing with the constitutional issues raised in the petition. The high court said that the petitioner should approach the Supreme Court of India with a petition as the Supreme Court had, on the administrative side, decided not to approve the authorisation of the Governor.

We approached the Supreme Court of India by filing a special leave petition against the high court order. We did lots of hard work and in-depth research, but the Supreme Court also dismissed the petition summarily. I failed again.

Recently, on 21st February 2025, on the international mother tongue day, I decided to launch a protest outside the High Court campus for not resolving our demand for allowing Gujarati as an official language in the Gujarat High Court proceeding in addition to English. I thought that this issue was not being taken up under competent leadership. I believe that if this issue was taken up by an abled leader, it would certainly bring the desired result. I took up the leadership without knowing whether I possessed leadership qualities. Ten days before the aforesaid day I constituted *"Uchch Nyalaya Matrubhasha Committee"*. I invited members of the bar all over Gujarat and people to join me in the protest on 21st February 2025. Many known and unknown people supported my demand on social media and expressed their willingness to join me in the protest. I applied for police permission to stage a protest outside Gujarat High Court. The police asked the number of persons likely to join the protest, to which I answered two hundred fifty. I thought all such people would support me by remaining present personally during the protest. We got sixty banners prepared with different slogans. We were fully ready to do a well-planned protest. All media persons were invited to take note of the protest. We gathered at the Gujarat High Court gate expecting a crowd surge. But hardly thirty-five advocates joined the protest. Out of the aforesaid thirty-five advocates, ten advocates were from a single office of Advocate Narendra Madhu, who I requested on the previous evening to join in my campaign when he came to brief me in one case. We shouted slogans for one hour and then dispersed. The aforesaid protest program could be described as a super flop show. I failed! But the media took this issue very seriously. To our good fortune, the news was flashed in the evening that the Home Minister had said that the government was serious about introducing the Gujarati language in the Gujarat High

Court as an additional language. So, the flop show turned out to be a matter of solace for all of us in the end.

I have failed so many times that now such failures do not deter my spirit. I realised that barring citizens of India and trial court lawyers, everyone else, viz. the lawyers of the high court, Supreme Court, and judges, are against the introduction of a regional language in the high court proceeding, even though in four states, viz. Bihar, Madhya Pradesh, Rajasthan, and Uttar Pradesh, Hindi is permitted as an official language in addition to English. I am, therefore, waiting for a political solution to the issue very soon. If that does not work, we can still approach the Supreme Court of India under Article 32 of the Constitution of India for enforcing the authorisation issued by the Governor in the year 2012 under Article 348(2) of the constitution. I am in hibernation at present but have not given up the fight for the Gujarati language.

Chapter 18

— ❖ —

Challenged Certain Instances of Injustice at Personal Costs

I do not remember, but maybe sometime in the year 2007-2008, one judge of the high court suddenly issued a fiat that henceforth no joint petition filed by more than one petitioner should be entertained. The High Court registry was directed to insist that the advocate should file a separate petition for each petitioner. Our obedient Bar started following the direction issued by that particular judge without any protest and without examining the legality of such a direction issued by the judge concerned. I felt that the insistence of filing a separate petition for each petitioner was absolutely unwarranted and most reprehensible. I, therefore, made research on the subject and wrote an article "A joint petition or a separate petition! – A legal labyrinth" and criticised the direction issued by the judge concerned. I gave reasons for my objections against the direction in the aforesaid article.

However, the practice of filing a separate petition for each petitioner legally entitled to file a single joint petition continued for more than a year and a half. Finally, a day came when I could challenge the aforesaid direction by filing a petition. The petition was listed before justice C.K. Buch. He expressed surprise as to how such a direction could be issued! He then asked me the reason why nobody had objected to such a direction issued by the judge concerned for almost one and a half years. I said that every stakeholder was happy with the

163

requirement of filing a separate petition. The judge asked me how could it be? I answered that the advocate for the petitioner was happy as he could quote a separate fee for each petitioner, his clerk would get his charges for each petition, the Government Pleader's office was also happy as each Assistant Government Pleader would get a separate fee for each petition and most importantly the judges were also happy as separate petitions would be disposed of by a common order/judgement that would add to his disposal of cases and improve his disposal ratio. Surprisingly, sometimes judges would dispose of separate petitions on the first day itself of their listing by passing an order that all the disposed of petitions would be governed by the order that would be passed in the main petition. What a fraud!

During the hearing of the case, justice C. K. Buch asked me to wait for a day. He said that he would speak to the Chief Justice and bring a solution, or else he would pass a judicial order. On the next day when the case was listed before justice C. K. Buch, I expressed my gratitude to him because on the previous evening the high court issued a circular clarifying that it would be permissible to file a joint petition for more than one person where facts are common and the relief is based on the common facts. I came out of the court jubilantly and attended court for the next couple of days in great elation for succeeding in getting rid of the unjust fiat issued by a particular judge.

The second instance of such a nature I could successfully nip in the bud. While I was the President of GHCAA the second time, one day in the evening a call came from the Chief Justice proposing to issue a notification/circular that from the next week all litigants and clerks would have to pay the court fee through electronic medium only. The physical court fee stamps would be done away with. I could not immediately respond to the proposal of the Chief Justice, but I only said for such a change to be implemented all concerned were required to be trained for at least three months to adapt to the new system. On that very evening, I did research on the modes of paying court fees. I noticed that the Gujarat Court Fees Act provided for paying court fees physically through court fee stamps and also electronically. I was excited to find such a provision in the court Fees Act. On the next day at 11 a.m., I met the Chief Justice and drew his attention to the aforementioned legal provision. He understood that only by amending the provisions of the Gujarat Court Fees Act was it possible to make it mandatory to make payment of court fees through electronic medium. He gave up the proposal, and I came out from his chamber victoriously as the implementation of his proposal would have created a controversy in the Bar. I was relieved from the stress of facing opposition from the members of the Bar and their clerks if the Chief Justice's whim was required to be implemented suddenly.

During the course of the hearing of one case, the Chief Justice expressed his unhappiness with the frequent filing of sick notes by advocates. He said that he would like to discontinue the practice of filing sick notes or leave notes by advocates. I was present in the courtroom. At that time, I was the President of the Bar, so I politely said that in the Gujarat High Court, apart from being a tradition to honour sick notes or leave notes, the High Court Rules, 1993 permitted the filing of a sick note or a leave note. I also pointed out the judgement of the Supreme Court on this point and convinced the Chief Justice not to change the longstanding convention and that particular Rule of the High Court Rules, 1993. I also pointed out that the judges, through their long experience, discern who is avoiding the hearing of a case by filing a sick note or leave note frequently or repeatedly and that he was entitled to curb such a tendency of a particular advocate by giving a very short adjournment. Thankfully, the Chief Justice gave up the idea of doing away with the Rule.

Similarly, on another day, the court wanted to restrain advocates other than a Senior Advocate from appearing and arguing a case on behalf of the advocate on record. Coincidentally, I was the President of the Bar at that time. I pointed out the provisions of the Civil Procedure Code which permit any advocate to argue and plead in a particular case upon the instruction of the advocate on record. Even a proxy slip was not necessary if the advocate on record is assisting during the hearing. The court was convinced. These are just a few instances of fighting against the establishment. These instances give me solace that I could seize every opportunity to do something for the Bar. I am indeed happy that I have at least succeeded to an extent in my efforts to prevent injustice.

◆◆

Chapter 19

Challenging the Practice of Casually Adjourning Bail Applications

One of my relatives was arrested for the violation of the provisions of the Gujarat Money Lenders Act in the year 2023. The violation amounted to a bailable offence. Other offences under the Indian Penal Code were inserted in the FIR just to justify his arrest and deny him bail. The graphic description of the chronology of events and the legal issues involved is set out hereunder.

On 02.12.2023, my relative was issued a summons by the investigating authority. The summons appeared to have been issued pursuant to a written complaint made by the original complainant, Mr. X. Due to the wedding of my relative's son, my relative requested the police to accommodate him and expressed his willingness to give his statement after the wedding.

My relative was issued another summons on 03.01.2023, which was obeyed by him, and he had cooperated in the inquiry/investigation.

An FIR was filed on 21.01.2023 for the offences punishable under Sections 40, 42(a), 42(d), 42(e), 44 of the Gujarat Money Lenders Act, 2011 (all offences are bailable) and under Section 384 (non-bailable), 114 & 506(1) of the Indian Penal Code, 1860.

On 21.01.2023, immediately after registration of the FIR, my relative was arrested within two hours of the registration of the FIR by abusing the power under Section 41 of Cr.PC and taken into police custody at 11.30 a.m. But the actual arrest was shown in the evening at 5 p.m. in violation of the mandate of law. On 22.01.2023, he was produced before the in-charge Magistrate since it was Sunday. Thereafter, the Magistrate concerned granted police custody of my relative for one day in violation of the provisions of Section 167 Cr.PC and directions issued in *Arnesh Kumar's* case even though no such police remand was sought by the police. On 23.01.2023, my relative was produced before the regular court. My relative preferred Regular Bail under Section 437 of Cr.P.C. However, instead of hearing the said bail application, the Magistrate sent my relative to judicial custody again in violation of the directions in *Arnesh Kumar's case* and adjourned the said Bail for hearing on 24.01.2023, upon a casual request made by the Public Prosecutor to call upon police papers. In fact, once the offences are punishable up to three years' imprisonment, no notice is necessary to the Public Prosecutor under Section 437 Cr.PC. However, the said adjournment was sought by the Public Prosecutor to facilitate the police to come with an additional report seeking insertion of Section 386 IPC, which is punishable with imprisonment up to ten years or more.

As per the well-thought plan on 24.01.2023, the investigating authority presented a report for the addition of an offence under Section 386 of the Indian Penal Code, 1860, before the Magistrate. It is pertinent to note that despite there being no allegations of Section 386 of the Indian Penal Code against my relative or any other accused, the said report was deliberately presented before the Magistrate as the punishment under the said offence was up to 10 years of imprisonment, in order to frustrate the law laid down in the case of *Arnesh Kumar* reported in *2014 (8) SCC 273* and *Satendar Kumar Antil* reported in *2022 (10) SCC 51*. The insertion of Section 386 IPC was an afterthought because the FIR was based on the written complaint of the informant and hence there was no possibility to miss any fact. Besides that, the

FIR appeared to have been preceded by a preliminary inquiry where the informant Mr. X had ample opportunity to state all facts. The preliminary inquiry seems to have preceded the FIR because my relative was issued two summonses prior to the registration of the FIR and that he had obeyed the summonses.

Thus, the arrest was made in contravention of the law laid down in *Arnesh Kumar* reported in *2014 (8) SCC 273* and *Satendar Kumar Antil* reported in *2022 (10) SCC 51* as the punishment in the present offence is below 7 years. The arrest of my relative was unwarranted since he had obeyed the summons and presented himself at the preliminary inquiry stage. It is only after my relative was sent to judicial custody that the offence under Section 386 of the Indian Penal Code, 1860, was sought to be added by way of a report. The said act of submitting the report for the addition of the offence was only subterfuge to avoid compliance with the clear and unequivocal directions of the hon'ble Supreme Court in *Arnesh Kumar (supra)*. In any case, the allegations sought to be added in the said report dated 24.01.2023 were only against accused no. 5 and not against my relative. Even a bare reading of the report made it clear that so far as the improved version was concerned, it also did not implicate my relative and did not satisfy the essential ingredients of Section 386 IPC.

The FIR seems to have been registered as a part of the drive initiated by the government to curb money lending without a licence, and it appears that the police authorities and even the judiciary were under instructions not to grant bail to the persons booked under the Gujarat Money Lenders Act. Several cases were filed during the years 2021 and 2022 that bear testimony to the fact that it was a special drive initiated by the state government. Other offences under the IPC invoked against my relative were punishable with a sentence of imprisonment of less than seven years. The law was settled long back in the year 2014 in the case of *Arnesh Kumar vs. State of Bihar* that the police should not arrest a person mechanically if the punishment prescribed for an offence is less than or up to seven years' imprisonment. This decision was not being implemented by police all over India, and therefore the Supreme Court took up the issue of illegal and unwarranted arrest again in *Satender Kumar Antil's* case. The Supreme Court issued a stern warning to police authorities not to transgress the constitutional limits and directed the police to follow the directions given in Arnesh Kumar's case in their letter and spirit. It was held by the Supreme Court that any violation of the directions would constitute contempt of court in addition to the liability under the service law. But these directions hardly reached the deaf ears of the police and trial courts, as can be seen from the facts unfolding hereafter.

Since it was a case involving my relative, I appeared in the Magistrate's court for the first time and argued at length. I drew the court's attention to the binding directions of the Supreme Court in *Arnesh Kumar* and *Satender Antil's* cases and urged the court to release my relative on bail. My relative had no antecedents of a criminal case. Moreover, most of the offences were bailable or punishable with less than seven years, making bail likely. The Magistrate denied bail without considering my arguments. We then approached the Sessions court hoping for a more favourable outcome. The Public Prosecutor did not argue against bail, leaving the decision to the court. We highlighted several cases under the Gujarat Money Lenders Act and IPC where bail or anticipatory bail had been granted. Unfortunately, my relative was denied bail. The saga continued as we turned to the high court. The high court issued a notice of one or two weeks to the state to respond, which was unnecessary according to the provisions of Section 439 Cr.PC and the High Court Rules, 1993. By the time the case was listed again, the court's roster had changed. It came before a judge known for being strict and slow in handling cases. He would adjourn bail applications for three to four weeks, waiting for the Public Prosecutor to finish other matters. At my insistence, he prioritised my case whenever it was listed. The case was heard intermittently for fifteen minutes each day over three days and then adjourned for four weeks for a final hearing, with a "Rule returnable" issued (a legal term indicating the case is set for final disposal). I was shocked and protested against this practice of issuing "Rule returnable" in bail matters right then in court. My relative's wife and family grew impatient as he had already spent over forty days in jail by the time the bail application was adjourned. By the returnable date, he would have been in jail for over sixty days. As per the court's practice, if a charge sheet is filed in the meantime, the applicant is sent back to the Sessions court to reapply for bail, further extending my relative's incarceration by twenty to thirty days. With no other recourse, my relative's family decided to settle with the informant by paying a substantial sum. After settling the case, we filed a quashing petition with the informant's consent. The quashing was granted, and my relative was released from jail after nearly sixty days of arrest, not on bail but because the FIR was quashed.

Since it was a political drive at one stage, the police threatened my relative's wife with her arrest. I filed a quashing petition for the wife and obtained a stay against her arrest. Undaunted by the Supreme Court's directions in *Arnesh Kumar* and *Satender Antil's* cases, the police proposed to invoke PASA (a preventive detention law) against my relative to keep him in jail if he was released on bail. I filed a petition at the pre-execution stage against the proposal to invoke PASA against him and got the stay.

Be that as it may, after detailed research, I wrote an article titled "Gujarat High Court's practice of issuing *"Rule Nisi"* in Bail Applications (posting bail applications for final hearing) Unknown to Law and Unconstitutional". I also made a representation to the Acting

Chief Justice through the GHCAA. But the practice of adjourning bail applications for three to four weeks by issuing "Rule returnable" continued up to August 2023. By that time, more than one thousand bail applications had piled up for final hearing. Upon repeated requests by me individually and the Bar Association, finally, all pending bail applications were assigned to four judges and were decided in a couple of months. However, the practice of issuing the Rule continued.

I was looking for an opportunity to espouse this issue on behalf of the undertrial prisoners. Fortunately, one client came to me who had been in jail for more than eighteen months, and his bail application in the high court had been adjourned twenty-seven times. I filed a petition addressing all legal and constitutional issues on his behalf without charging a fee. For the main bail application, I did charge him, but for this petition questioning the practice of issuing a Rule in bail matters and hearing them finally after three to four weeks, I did not charge him at all. When the aforementioned petition was listed for a hearing before the bench of the Chief Justice, the bench was surprised by such a practice. The bench decided the petition in favour of my client. The court stated that in bail matters, there was no question of adjourning it for a final hearing by issuing a Rule. The court emphasised that bail applications must be decided at the earliest as they pertain to the liberty of a person. The citation of the case is *Bhavesh Baldevbhai Desai/Rabari versus State of Gujarat 2024(2) GLH 231.*

The aforementioned judgement has also stopped the practice of relegating an applicant to the trial court for bail when a charge sheet is filed during the high court proceeding.

I am glad that the view canvassed by me was approved by the high court. This judgement is of seminal importance for the liberty of a person.

Chapter 20

Remembering Some Judges Doing Justice without Formalities

I would like to mention one instance, out of many, of a judge doing justice without insisting the advocate to do all formalities that are required for the listing of a case on board for hearing. It was a case where one company had called its annual general meeting at Bombay and all shareholders from different parts of India were to attend the meeting. There was one disgruntled director or a shareholder who did not want the general meeting of the company to be convened. He filed a Civil Suit in Vadodara Civil court and sought *ex parte* stay against the meeting though the suit was legally not maintainable in civil court. The only competent forum to adjudicate the legality of the meeting of the company was the tribunal (most probably at that time "Company Law Board") created under the Companies Act. The main purpose of filing a suit by that person was to cause embarrassment to the management and to wreak personal vengeance. The Vadodara Court granted stay and restrained the company from holding the meeting the next day. The company was served with a copy of the stay order just at 12 noon of the previous day of the proposed meeting leaving no room for the management of the company to challenge the order before the high court in the Gujarat state. In those days the only mode of quick communication of the order of the court and the relevant papers of the suit proceeding was a fax machine. I got a call from one of the directors of the company at 1 o'clock in the noon on the previous day of the meeting. He explained the situation and the embarrassment they were going to face the next day. I told the director that it was almost impossible to circulate an appeal or a petition in the high court on the same day and get a stay from the high court. I had received the information from the director at 1 p.m. and therefore a very short time was left for circulating the matter and list it on the same day. I said I would try my best but said that he should not be too optimistic. In those days in our court chamber there was no fax machine so I asked the clerk to go to our office five kilometres away to get those papers through fax. I got the papers during the recess. I cursorily browsed through the papers. At 2.30 after the court recess, I mentioned for the urgent circulation of the appeal before the Acting Chief Justice Mr. Justice C. K Thakker. I said that I wanted urgent circulation of an appeal but said that I had no copy of the order, I had no Vakalatnama of the client, I had no papers pertaining to the suit and that it was not possible for me to get an affidavit of the client in support of the proceedings before the high court. The court understood the mischief played by one director/shareholder who had obtained the stay against holding of the annual general meeting in Bombay from the Vadodara Court which had no jurisdiction. The Acting Chief Justice simply asked me to write down whatever I mentioned orally and get it typed on one page. He permitted the listing of the matter on the same day dispensing with the filing of Vakalatnama, certified copy of the order, affidavit in support of our stay application and filing of the papers of the suit proceeding. He told me to mention the matter before the concerned judge having the roster of hearing civil appeals. Fortunately, the judge concerned was Justice Mr. A. R Dave. My task was easy as the Acting Chief Justice had permitted me to circulate the appeal on the same day at 4 p.m. subject to the convenience of the judge concerned. I in the midst of the ongoing matter mentioned the matter before justice A.R. Dave tendering apology for interjecting during the hearing of another case. Justice Dave appreciated the fact and expressed surprise as to how Vadodara Court could grant such a stay against holding of an annual general meeting of a company in Bombay! At 4 p.m. the appeal was listed by the High Court registry after giving it a filing number. The court had understood the case during the mentioning of the matter and hence asked me two three factual questions and granted a stay against the Vadodara Court order and pending proceeding before the said court. I could not believe the happening of an impossible thing and came out of the court triumphantly. It was a glorious victory. When I conveyed the order to the directors of the company, they were also pleasantly surprised by my carrying out the mission successfully. They came down to Ahmedabad from Bombay to personally congratulate me and saving them from embarrassment and humiliation by one disgruntled shareholder/director. I said that the entire credit goes to the learnt Acting Chief Justice who allowed me circulation of the appeal by jettisoning all formalities for the cause of substantial justice.

This episode I am writing in this book for the knowledge of the judges currently occupying the chair of justice and those persons going to become judges so that they can emulate justice C K Thakker. I have noticed a tendency of the judges sacrificing substantial justice for procedural formalities. They forget very quickly their own difficulties as an advocate in filing a case in the registry and getting the case listed urgently on the same day or on the next day. I hope in all suitable and urgent cases judges must be concerned with doing substantial justice relaxing all procedural obstacles and learn from the above example. Similarly, in another case in a matter pertaining to several workmen, the President of a Municipality who had ceased to be the office bearer entered into an illegal settlement with the workmen and the lawyer of the workmen. The settlement was recorded by Justice Mr. H.K Rathod and he passed the order directing reinstatement of the workmen in service. The judge was not made aware of the fact that the person who represented as President had ceased to be the President. The fact came to the knowledge of the municipality within one hour of the passing of the order. The municipality contacted me and apprised me of the fact that the person representing as President was no longer the President of the municipality and the settlement was fraud. During the course of the same day, I mentioned the fact to justice Rathod and apprised him of the correct facts and that a fraud was committed by the parties. I sought circulation of an application for recalling the order and staying the order. I was granted permission to circulate the application on the same day by the judge without insisting on any formality of a supporting affidavit, requirement of Vakalatpatra etc. He stayed his own order before the order based on the illegal settlement reached the municipality officially. There are many instances where we had completed two rounds of litigations the same day in the high court. That could happen because the judges were more interested in doing substantial justice than insisting the advocate to go through the procedural formalities.

Nowadays, I am really shocked and surprised by the usual reply received from a judge to a request made by an advocate for urgent circulation that the advocate should convince the registry and only after completion of all formalities the matter would be listed on the board. I am not saying that in all cases urgent circulation is to be granted. But I do believe that in deserving cases, the court must grant circulation of a case on the same day or the next day without insisting on completing formalities. It is often said that procedural requirements should be considered to be a handmaid and not to be treated as the mistress. But now unfortunately procedural requirements have overshadowed their subservient role and assumed the role of the mistress.

Chapter 21

A Letter to Chief Justice Cost Me More Than
One Lakh Rupees

While I was holding the post of the President of the Bar Association somewhere in the year 2016-17 I received many complaints that some judges had a tendency of reserving judgement after the conclusion of arguments and not pronouncing reserved judgements for more than six months. I had also faced such a situation in one urgent tender and contract matter when I was not a Senior Advocate. In my case, the judge concluded the hearing and adjourned the matter for order. I waited for more than three months in the hope that the matter would be listed for order, but it was not being listed on the daily board. Whenever I sent my clerk to the High Court registry to find out the status of the case, no satisfactory answer was given by the registry. Since four months had passed and, in the meantime, I received many complaints from the members of the Bar that many judges had developed this habit of indefinitely delaying the pronouncement of judgements. So, I wrote a letter to the then Chief Justice by citing the Supreme Court's judgement in *Anil Rai vs State of Bihar AIR 2001 SC 3173* on the issue of the desirability of the early pronouncement of a judgement. The Supreme Court had issued detailed directions in the aforesaid judgement about the course to be adopted by an advocate when a judge fails to pronounce judgement within a reasonable time. In the letter to the Chief Justice, I requested that this letter be circulated to all judges for their knowledge and to do the needful.

After the circulation of the aforesaid letter to all judges, those judges who were delaying the pronouncement of judgement started pronouncing judgements. I was informed that in one month after the aforesaid letter, at least thirty-five judgements were pronounced by the judges concerned. But the aforesaid letter had no impact on the judge who had kept my urgent case pending for more than six months.

In the meantime, it so happened that I had argued one case before another judge and that matter was pending for judgement for the last two months. This judge took the letter personally upon him and felt that the letter was targeted at him. I got the news that the judge started criticising my letter and said in the open court that Mr. Pandya should give the names of the judges who were delaying the pronouncement of judgements and it should not be left to guesswork. It was a case with a chequered history where about thirteen cases between the same parties were clubbed together. I was the advocate only in one case out of thirteen where I had filed a caveat two years back. The judge concerned tagged all thirteen cases together and listed them on a particular day. The judge started calling all advocates to appear before him and one of them was me. The judge asked me the reason for filing a caveat as there were many things in the case that intrigued the judge about the bona fide of the litigation. In open court, I gave the reasons for filing a caveat and told that it was a case referred to me by a recently made Senior Advocate. I casually said that ordinarily at the time of filing a caveat nobody applies his mind to the merit of the case. Most of the time caveats are filed in a routine manner. The judge was perhaps of the belief that there was no need for me to have filed a caveat as the judgement appealed before the high court did not adversely affect my client's legal interest. I thought that I had given proper justification for accepting the case referred to me by a Senior Advocate two years back. On the next day, I was asked to complete my arguments and again clarify the reason for filing a caveat. I tried to contact the clients but their mobile was switched off. So, on the next day, I informed the judge accordingly and made submissions for the clients I was engaged without knowing much about the chequered history of the case and the parties. I hardly made oral arguments for more than five minutes and forgot that the group of thirteen cases remained pending for the next two months without delivering a judgement. It was learnt that after my arguments were concluded two Senior Advocates appearing in the said group of cases made submissions vehemently personally against me behind my back. They maligned me to the best of their ability since they knew that the judge hearing the case wanted such allegations to be made against me. Trying to please a judge for personal benefit forgetting all propriety is a trait of many advocates everywhere. Anyway, I have accepted the truth that these are weaknesses of greedy advocates.

After about one week of my aforementioned letter to the Chief Justice, this judge also pronounced judgement in the group of thirteen cases. He dug out the details of when I filed a caveat, which judge was assigned the roster of the case at that time and on the basis of his groundwork drew an adverse inference against me. In the judgement, he made certain adverse remarks running in four paragraphs against my conduct of accepting the case and said that I tried to indulge in forum shopping, which was not true. However, knowing me and my reputation as a straightforward advocate, he gave the benefit of doubt to me after making insinuations against me. Be that as it may, I was hurt by these insinuations.

The true story is that two years back I received a call from a then made a Senior Advocate that he would like to refer one matter to me as he was appearing for some other parties to the litigation and he would not be able to represent the client referred to me by him. These things happen many times in legal profession. I thought that a new avenue of getting cases had opened up for me and got tempted by it. He asked me whether I was taking up cases that may be listed before justice A J Desai as he knew that Mr. Desai was my cousin. I said that if Justice Desai had issued a notice in the matter or had ever applied his judicial mind to the case or if he had kept the matter part-heard, I do not accept the case dealt with by Justice Desai at any point of time. The reason for refusing such matters is obvious that many a time litigants want to avoid a particular judge for some personal benefit and I never allowed such tactics played by litigants or lawyers. The Senior Advocate said that the matter was only once listed before Justice Desai in the defect list where a general order was passed that defects to be removed within two weeks and that Justice Desai had not applied his judicial mind to the case. I again reconfirmed from the Senior Advocate whether Justice Desai had ever taken up any of the cases of that party in the past and for that reason the litigant is trying to avoid his case being taken up by Justice Desai. He said that no such thing had happened in the past. The Senior Advocate assured me that he would be leading the matter and I was to just appear for the supporting respondent. He sent his junior and the client with a huge bunch of a file, caveat and Vakalatnama. On that day I was busy in the meeting with another client when the junior of the aforesaid Senior Advocate and client came with the case papers and fee. I said that the cheque be given to my receptionist and he should simply put a tick-mark against the name of the party who I was to represent as my ongoing meeting was likely to take long. My clerk filed the caveat. In the said matter there were several respondents and it so happened that whenever the case was listed any one would seek an adjournment. The case remained pending for two years without even admission hearing and rotated before different judges who were assigned such cases by the roster fixed by Chief Justice. None of the parties showed willingness to proceed with the matter before any judge. Finally, the one particular judge who I referred to above decided to take up the aforesaid case and all allied matter between the same parties in respect of the same subject matter. As said earlier I was called by the judge to argue the case as other advocates had substantially argued the case by the time I was called. I asked for adjournment as I was unaware of the ongoing hearing of the case. The judge asked me what was my stand in the case and to clarify on the next day why did I choose to file a caveat. I tried to contact the client referred to by the Senior Advocate but he was not reachable. On the next day I explained to the judge that I had received the case through one Senior Advocate and that the caveat was filed in a routine manner. I clarified my legal stand in the matter. Since my reputation as a lawyer is very good the judge did not bother me further and I thought that he had believed what I had explained to him.

But to my misfortune, the judge took my letter to the Chief Justice and made adverse remarks against me. I got really disturbed and realised that I was used by the Senior Advocate who sent me the client, and I fell prey to his shoddy court craft. I would like to partly blame myself also as I did not realise the plan of the Senior Advocate and did not pay attention to the merit of the case before filing a caveat. The only possible intention of the Senior Advocate was that since Justice Desai was very quick in understanding the cases listed before him, he might decide the case on the very day of the listing whereas all the parties wanted to keep the litigation pending for a long time in the high court for reasons best known to them.

Be that as it may, I thought to file a review application before the same judge but someone advised me not to do that as he would make more comments on me. So, I decided to file a petition in the Supreme Court. The law on the subject is very clear that no adverse comment can be made against a party, an advocate or a subordinate judge without giving the person concerned an opportunity of hearing. I was never put to notice that the judge was proposing to make adverse comments against me. The law is clear that where a tribunal consists of one judge only, no relative of such judge can file appearance in the case going to be listed before him. Where there is a possibility to assign the case to another judge, the aforesaid restriction would not apply. I had accepted a self-imposed restriction that wherever Justice Desai had applied his judicial mind or dealt with the matter judicially during his roster or any previous bail application had been disposed of by him, I would refuse to file my appearance as an advocate for any party. Anyway, I filed a petition in the Supreme Court and requested Senior Advocate Mr. Arvind Datar, Advocate Mr. Amar Dave, advocate Ms. Aishwarya Bhati and AOR Purvish Malkan to take care of the case and get the remarks expunged. The matter was adjourned from time to time in the Supreme Court. One bench was about to expunge the remarks against me but the Senior Advocate who had perhaps objected to my judgeship was coincidentally appearing for one of the parties and he took serious objection against the expunction of remarks. The matter got adjourned at his instance. Thus, I must have travelled to Delhi more than five times for expunging remarks made in the judgement by the high court and incurred expenses of more than one lakh rupees on travelling and hotel stay. All the advocates referred to above agreed to appear for me without charging a fee. However, during Covid time, the matter was listed for virtual hearing. I approached Mr. Yatin Oza and said that the matter was listed for hearing if he could make some arrangement for a Supreme Court Senior Advocate. He asked me the details of the case and the bench before which it was to be listed and said he would appear for me if I did not mind. I said yes as I knew that Mr. Oza had a very good rapport with the bench before which my matter was going to be listed so I was sure that the court would give a patient hearing to Mr. Oza. He appeared and convinced the judge to expunge the remarks. The judges were kind to agree to expunge adverse remarks made against me. It was also pointed out by Mr. Oza that I had been designated as a Senior Advocate in the meantime lending credibility to my blamelessness. I am indeed grateful to all the aforesaid advocates who helped me take care of my matter in the Supreme Court and indebted to Mr. Yatin Oza forever. But the net result of my letter is that the letter to the Chief Justice cost me more than one lakh rupees. If I had not written the aforesaid letter, I am sure that the judge concerned would not have made any adverse remarks against me. Anyway, all is well that ends well. In fact, if we see the remarks made by the judge concerned, they were not serious. He had also given the benefit of doubt to me for such a deviation but I took it very seriously.

Another folly I did is challenging the adverse remarks by filing a special leave petition in the Supreme Court. During the same period, the very same judge had made serious adverse remarks against the Advocate General Mr. Kamal Trivedi who got the adverse remarks expunged by filing an intra-court appeal in the same court by taking a practical route. My studious mind decided that an intra-court appeal in my case would not be maintainable because the case where I appeared was originating from the civil trial proceeding. If I had filed an intra-court appeal without being too technical, perhaps the appellate bench would have expunged the remarks, ignoring the question of the maintainability of the proceeding. Now I realise that sometimes it is wise to be practical rather than being too bookish. But things done cannot be undone. I was too late to get this wisdom.

Chapter 22

A Judge Defying His Proposed Transfer Was Rewarded with Supreme Court Judgeship

A judge who did not allow my urgent tender petition to be listed on board for passing the final order for six months and who was proposed to be transferred to another high court to the utter shock to me and the entire legal fraternity was elevated as a judge of the Supreme Court later on. As stated in an earlier chapter that my letter raising a grievance of some judges not pronouncing judgements quickly after the conclusion of the hearing of a case was essentially targeted at this particular judge. It was written for a few other judges also known for not pronouncing judgements quickly. The judge for whom the letter to the Chief Justice was written was unperturbed. I have firsthand knowledge that this judge kept the file pertaining to my tender/contract matter in his chamber for approximately six months and did not send it back to the registry after it was adjourned on the last date of its listing. I specifically pointed out that my aforesaid case was not listed for the last six months after it was adjourned. I drew the attention of the Chief Justice that my matter was very urgent and could not brook any delay. I stated that the case needed to be disposed of one way or the other and it could not be kept pending for no reasons. I made this complaint to the Chief Justice in the morning at 11 A.M and at 2.30 P.M the case file was sent back to the registry for its listing on the next day. This leads to a conclusion that the Chief Justice told the judge concerned about my complaint since both were under the zone of consideration for elevation as Judge Supreme Court. My complaint would have marred the chances of the judge concerned of his elevation. So, he immediately sent back the file to the registry. I have proof of the file movement register showing that the judge concerned kept the case file with him for six months and it was sent back on the day when I made a complaint to the Chief Justice. The matter was listed on the next day before the bench concerned taking up the tender and contract cases but was adjourned at the instance of one of the respondents. After a week, the roster got changed and the matter was assigned to the same judge against whom I had made a complaint. When the case was called out for hearing, the judge concerned started hearing the case as if nothing had happened. I raised a strong objection against the said judge taking up the case for hearing and requested the judge to recuse himself from the case. He understood what I was conveying to him. He reluctantly recused himself from the hearing of my aforesaid case. A legal inference has to be drawn from the sequence of events that the judge concerned was influenced by some extraneous considerations. Otherwise, why should a judge do the things not usually done!

The Supreme Court was aware of this incident. Besides the aforesaid incident, there was already a proposal of his transfer to another high court pending before the government. But the aforesaid judge was in the good books of the ruling party. The ruling party was not willing to implement the recommendation of the Supreme Court collegium to transfer the aforesaid judge to another high court as a pusine judge. The then Chief Justice of India expressed his anguish openly in the media and declared that if the judge concerned was not transferred as per the recommendation of the collegium, he would withdraw judicial work from him. But nothing happened to the judge concerned. He was later made Chief Justice of one high court and then elevated as a judge,

Supreme Court of India! Thus, the judge who defied his transfer from one high court to another was rewarded with judgeship in Supreme Court of India. This is how our system of appointment to the superior court and transfer of judges from one high court to another high court functions! This instance is narrated just to point out the flaws in our system of appointment and transfer of a judge of a superior court. The judge concerned against whom I had written the above-mentioned complaint was once upon a time my good friend having been appointed as Central government Standing Counsels simultaneously by the same notification. After the aforesaid episode our relationship got strained. He is now retired. I have given up the feeling of resentment towards him because by now I have realised that this is how the legal system functions in our country.

During my thirty-five years of career as an advocate, I could successfully get transferred one judge who used to do justice with a predetermined mind and who would not allow a lawyer to argue his case in his own manner. At one stage of my career as an advocate, I found that a few judges who were proposed by the Supreme Court collegium to be transferred to other high courts but were not transferred by the government for political reasons. I, therefore, wrote a letter to the Chief Justice of India to make those judges sit in a bench of two judges so as to make them ineffective and indirectly achieve the proposed transfer through judicial means. I presume that the Chief Justice of India, to my surprise, immediately acted upon my letter. Just within three days of my writing a letter to the CJI, the roster of the High Court of Gujarat was changed and those judges facing transfer were made to sit as a pusine judge in benches of two judges! I had nothing personal against those judges. Some of them are really good to me but I was more interested in seeing that the rule of law and constitution should prevail. My personal rapport with those judges was immaterial.

Chapter 23

The Bar Showed Solidarity Against the Mala Fide Transfer of an Independent Judge

As stated earlier, I have failed to understand the functioning of the collegium system. The example of a proposed transfer of a newly appointed but independent judge would demonstrate how extraneous factors play an important role in the decision-making process of the collegium system. The members of the Bar were very happy with the working of one particular judge as he was fearless and independent. He was relief-oriented and would try to give relief to a litigant within the four corners of the law. In short, he believed in doing substantial justice rather than being bogged down by technicalities. In short, to the best of the information available to me, there was no adverse material against him which would necessitate his transfer.

Despite the aforementioned favourable facts, one day the news flashed on the Bar & Bench and Live Law news reporting platform that there was a proposal to transfer this judge. It was shocking because there were no complaints against this judge. When I reached court, I expressed shock about the proposal of transfer of this judge at the meeting place in the high court known as South Concourse where lawyers gather in the morning at 10.30 before court work commences. I could not digest this news and hence typed a WhatsApp message that the proposed transfer of a very good judge strikes at the independence of the judiciary and exhorted every advocate to protest the transfer. The message became viral. The first advocate who supported my message was Mr. Yatin Oza, Senior Advocate. Others started supporting my message and within no time the Bar was unanimous to protest the proposed transfer. At the South Concourse of the High Court, we discussed the method of protest. It struck to my mind that the strike was not an option in view of the Supreme Court judgements and hence we had to find out a new tool of protest. I proposed that let all advocates gather in the Chief Justice's court at 12 noon and if the Chief Justice asked the reason for thronging into his court, we should say that we had gathered here to mourn the death of the independence of the judiciary. We all decided that Mr. Mihir Thakore being the senior most amongst us would speak if the Chief Justice asked the reason for all advocates gathering in his court. I circulated the message in one or two WhatsApp groups that all advocates should reach the Chief Justice's court at 12 noon sharp and requested all group members to circulate this message in other groups. At 12 noon, advocates started pouring into the Chief Justice's court and in no time the courtroom was houseful! The Chief Justice was taken aback by this sudden surge of advocates in his courtroom. As anticipated, he asked us the reason for gathering in his court and Mr. Mihir Thakore politely said that we had gathered there to mourn the death of the independence of the judiciary. He said we would observe two minutes of silence and disperse. This incident was reported in all news portals. The message reached the Supreme Court loud and clear and the proposal to transfer that judge was put off. Later on, it is learnt that probably the aforesaid judge was to be transferred at the instance of one Supreme Court Judge who had an axe to grind against him, an independent judge.

In my view, it was a great victory to restore judicial independence and the rule of law in the deteriorating judicial system. During the same time, a proposal to transfer another good judge resurrected for reasons best known to the Supreme Court collegium. I tried to garner support from the members of the Bar against his transfer also, but unfortunately, the Bar was not unanimous. I failed again!

Epilogue

Today, whether somebody recognises me as a successful person or not, I feel myself successful for doing many adventurous acts. To me success means fighting against injustice irrespective of the outcome. I have not only fought against whatever instances of injustice I encountered during my professional life but tried to make the legal profession and judicial system a little better than what it was before I joined the profession. Even otherwise, I considered myself successful because I am bestowed with a life I had never dreamt of. I am lucky and successful in creating my own worth or value in the profession of law through which I have been able to fulfil most of my family's mundane desires. I feel truly fulfilled by doing all the above-mentioned experiments in my life. Whatever I thought appropriate at a particular stage of my life, I did it without bothering about the consequences thereof. Possibly that is the reason why I feel fully contented. God keeps on giving opportunities to everyone to do something for the larger benefit but, most of us fail to grab such opportunities. I am glad that I have seized every such opportunity to bring reforms in the legal system at the cost of my personal loss. I am still willing and eager to experiment more adventures or you may call misadventures as and when a situation would demand me to do so. As stated in the Prologue, I firmly believe in what Osho said "Do not call it insecurity, call it freedom. Do not call it uncertainty, call it wonder". Today I am a man who has all the freedom to live life dangerously and enjoy the thrill of my every action.

Lastly, I would like to express my special thanks to late Justice Mr. Ghanshym Udhwani (to me Ghanumal), Percy Kavina, Mukesh A. Patel, Yogesh Thakkar, Dhaval Dave, my cousin Ashish Desai (Retd. Chief Justice Kerala High Court), Premal Nanavati, Amee Yajnik, Stayajeet Desai, Saurin Mehta, Hardik Rawal, Asutosh Shastri (Retired Judge, Gujarat High Court), Vipul Pancholi (now Judge High Court), Vaibahvi Nanvati (now Judge High Court), Devang Nanvati, Sanjeev Dave and Udayan Vyas for being good friends and part of my professional journey. I am indeed grateful to my mentors/seniors viz. Late Senior Advocate Mr. K. G. Vakharia, Senior Advocate Mr. Yatin Oza, Justice A. R. Dave (Retd. Judge Supreme Court), Senior Advocate Mr. S.I. Nanvati and all others, including the unnamed senior of the city civil court Ahmedabad, who all guided me in the profession or made me explore the profession in my own way. I am immensely thankful to Mr. Vijay Patel for inducting me as his partner in his law firm, allowing me complete freedom to run the firm for seventeen years. I am thankful for all my present and past juniors in the office namely Manan Bhatt, Jay Sunilbhai Shah, Shyam Shah, Gaurav Vyas, Tejal Doshi, Femina Chapatwala, Kanan Rawal, Kruti G. Shah, Avani Thaker, Utkarsh Sharma, Harshil Shukla, Suresh Bhatt, Sushil Shukla, Shirish Patel, Dhaval Vakil (Patel), Dishant Thakkar, Hina Raval, Rimpal Patel, Anmol Surelia, Renisha Vyas, Rini Tripathi, Kartik Pandya, Rakesh Sharma, Alkesh Shah, Chetnaben Shah. I firmly believe that through their existence I got opportunity to improve my performance in court hearings as an advocate and I became a senior in true sense.

Finally, I wish life would unfold more and more opportunities in my remaining professional journey to do something better for society. Failing multiple times has become part of me and I learn many new things from every failure.